Faces of Metanoia

God's Call to Life-Changing Relationship in the Lives of
Francis of Assisi, Clare of Assisi
Dorothy Day, and Oscar Romero

Gillian T.W. Ahlgren

VITALITY
buzz, bliss + books

Faces of Metanoia: God's Call to Life-Changing Relationship
in the Lives of Francis of Assisi, Clare of Assisi, Dorothy Day,
and Oscar Romero
Copyright © 2026 by Gillian T. W. Ahlgren
Published by VITALITY buzz, bliss + books LLC
vitalitybuzz.org

VITALITY buzz, bliss + books LLC publishes original creations to
grow the mission of VITALITY Cincinnati Inc, a 501(c)3 education-
based nonprofit: sharing holistic self-care from neighborhood to
neighborhood, person to person, and breath by breath since 2010.

The opinions and ideas expressed herein are those of the author
and do not necessarily represent the opinions of the VATRONS of
VITALITY buzz, bliss + books LLC or the Board of Trustees of
VITALITY Cincinnati. Any errors, of course, are solely the author's.

Every effort has been made to give credit to other people's original
ideas through the text itself. If you feel something should be credited
to someone and is not, please get in touch through our website and
every effort will be made to correct this text for future printings.
Thank you!

Gillian is grateful to dear friend Nancy Bradley for greatly improving
this book.

We invite you to honor your mind, your body, your whole self. Do
only what you know to be right for you. While the invitations offered
here in this book, on our websites and social media, and in our classes
are geared to be gentle and easily modified by the participant to fit
the participants' needs, please consult your medical doctor or health
professional before undertaking any practices.

ISBN: 978-1-954688-43-8

Contemplative
Wisdom for
Today

CONTENTS

About This Book

We know that the God of life calls us into relationship. And we know that relationship with God has the capacity to change everything. But we don't always live into the life-changing relationship that life-with-God is. In this book, I put four faces to the phenomenon of metanoia—God's call to life-changing relationship—so that we can consider what collaboration with God has looked like in past eras and what it might look like today. The lives and teachings of four friends of God—Francis of Assisi, Clare of Assisi, Dorothy Day, and Oscar Romero—all of whom provide stellar examples of fidelity to God and visionary spiritual leadership, can provide us much food for thought.

Although I intentionally use recognizable "faces" of metanoia drawn from the Christian tradition, I want to make clear that metanoia is a genuine process of searching, a journey that is likely to lead to new ways of experiencing what it is to be human and what it is to be related to other people. As I review the lives of Francis, Clare, Dorothy Day, and Oscar Romero, I identify specific moments of encounter, choice and commitment that each of them experienced. I consider these to be "moments of metanoia"—that is, moments that evoked responses in them and led each of them through successive stages of growth in their friendship and collaboration with God. With each life, we can ask whether or not we, too, have had moments similar to the ones that were so significant for Francis of Assisi, Clare of Assisi, Dorothy Day, and Oscar Romero.

I am structuring this exploration of metanoia in each life according to a five-step process that first emerged organically for me as I considered the lives of Francis and Clare. Since the process of metanoia is unique to each person, these five stages will never appear in exactly the same way in a person's life, and, in some cases, the stages themselves may not differentiate into discrete and separable moments. My point is not to force characterizations on the experience of metanoia. But exploring metanoia as a sequential process marked by growth and ongoing change can help us in two ways. First, it enables us to see what becomes possible as we orient ourselves to life with God and build accountability into our relationship with God. Second, and more fundamentally, it highlights the centrality of Jesus's ministry to draw people on the path toward greater goodness, individually and communally. Because each of these four figures was deeply committed to embodying the way of Jesus that the gospels convey, observing their development can help us find our own places in a relational narrative that transcends time and space.

The five sequential phases of metanoia that we will consider in each life are:

An Unexpected Invitation: how the events of life, especially those that disrupt our trajectories, can sometimes contain unexpected lessons and graces that make us pause and even change course,

Eyes to See: how others, especially those at the margins, often help us examine the world from alternate perspectives and experiences, giving us a greater sense of what is not working in our world; indeed, our connections with others show us how life is made richer and more fulfilling as we collaborate to make a world that is home for all,

Radical Departure/Beyond Barriers: how the deepening sense of what really matters emerging from our growing solidarity with others often calls us to choose away from social and cultural norms, in order to move beyond the expectations of society and toward communities that mirror those that Jesus created,

Radiating Love: our deeper practical exploration of communities of care that make the love of God palpable and that inspire others to live with greater integrity and purity of heart,

The Revolution of Tenderness: how our lives, individually and communally, generate a revolution of tenderness across time and space, and how we attend to the ongoing presence of lovingkindness in the world, even once we have left this earth.

Reflective prompts are included around each of these "moments" in the lives of Francis, Clare, Dorothy Day, and Oscar Romero that will help you consider the uniqueness of each life and also how you, too, may have experienced these moments. In each chapter, you are encouraged to consider what these moments would look like for you in this time and place.

Our review of their lives will also enable us to see how such moments of metanoia begin to shape a life of metanoia—that is, a life of malleability and transformation that the invitation to partnership with God actually requires of us. Together, these figures will show us how metanoia, then and now, is a life of openness to active participation in the Love that supports, encourages, restores and reshapes a hurting world.

This book is intended to be used in conjunction with a journal or notebook where you can engage the prompts and write about any and everything in these narratives that speaks to the hungers of your heart. This book can also be used in small faith-sharing groups and reading groups, where it is safe to explore what you are noticing as you proceed. A bibliography for further reading and exploration is included at the end.

If you are interested in a "Faces of Metanoia" retreat and/or an introduction to the book for reading circles, please contact the author at ahlgren@xavier.edu.

Introduction:
What is Metanoia?

METANOIA

A thorough and holistic process of change, rooted in a deepening relationship with God and a concurrent commitment to goodness.

A coherent and compelling process that we undergo as we place our whole selves in the service of something more than ourselves.

The change in our hearts, choices, and actions that we embrace as part of a rich, intricate, and fragile web of life.

You may not know exactly what the word "metanoia" means, but if you feel discouraged, disheartened, or overwhelmed by life in today's world, it is quite possible that part of you already yearns for it. Looking out at our world, it is hard not to see the missed opportunities, lack of collaboration, willful abandonment of principles, needless cruelty, and growing fatalism that tempts us to think that there is little we can do to change the reckless chaos around us. But we are not the first generation in need of a reset. The real question is: Will we have the wisdom and humility to implement meaningful change that frees all of us to be better people? If this is what we truly want, then we cannot settle for anything less than the path of metanoia, illuminated by those who have explored it before us.

Metanoia is a profound change of mind, heart, attitude, orientation and action that is guided by our growing alignment with what we understand God's desire, for us and from us, to be. Metanoia is a both a committed and ongoing response to the vitalizing love of God and a journey propelled by that same love that draws us toward our capacity and giftedness, allowing us to share ourselves in ways we cannot imagine on our own.

Metanoia involves a shift in perspective, disposition, practice and habit, informed by a deepening relationship with God. Rather than a one-time event, metanoia is an ongoing process whose beauty and depth reveals itself over time, a multi-faceted transformation toward greater goodness that creates possibility. Metanoia is what John the Baptist announced and Jesus taught and embodied—a movement out of self, with a new orientation to God that gives us a new vision of a human community in which God would feel welcome. In short, metanoia is the invitation to life-changing relationship with the divine—a journey that, for each of us, is unique.

When searching for a basic definition of metanoia, you may find the word translated linguistically and conceptually as "conversion." This synonym is a poor launching pad for our exploration, for several reasons. First, it is incomplete linguistically, particularly when it suggests a one-time, life-changing event. As our figures will demonstrate, even when we can point to very clear "moments of metanoia" in a person's life, such moments are embedded in a much larger and more intricate relational tapestry—a web, if you will, of relationships, with God at the center of everything, but our relationship with self and others is intertwined with that relationship with God.

One of the twentieth-century theologians who spent significant time and energy embedding the role of conversion into a larger process of self-transcendence was Bernard Lonergan. According to Lonergan, the point of Christianity and even of human existence, was continual self-transcendence. Lonergan understood this process as one of ongoing conversion and movement toward honesty and authenticity as a human being. Conversion, for Lonergan, had little to do with religious identity; rather it entailed our broadening vista and perspective, or, as he put it, our movement toward horizons that enabled us to envision possibility, guided by our continual engagement of relationship with God. In other words, as we walk more deeply with God, what matters to us begins to change, and, more importantly, what and how we see, in the world around us, broadens and deepens. We might think of this as broadening our horizons, but we can also think of it as entering new realms of possibility as we continually move toward the possibilities that life with God offers us.

Lonergan also developed a helpful framework for understanding conversion to operate on multiple levels—the intellectual, the moral, the affective, the psychological, and the religious, to name a few. Appreciating the many dimensions of conversion, as Lonergan explains it, can be useful in our appreciation of metanoia, which leaves no part of our lives unchanged. Finally, Lonergan encouraged people to think about conversion as a movement from a way of being toward a different way of being; in introducing Lonergan's thought, scholars and educators often discuss "conversion from" and "conversion to." For example, we would contrast self-absorption with self-transcendence, lovelessness with love and tenderness, selfishness and greed with generosity and moral rectitude.

But here is where the translation of metanoia as "conversion" begins to fall apart, particularly when it contains no intrinsic relational foundation and does not expose us, directly and deeply, to the God of life and love. In reality, we need experiential knowledge of the love of God if we are to have any chance of embodying and incarnating love in the world around us. Since it is love that fuels metanoia, we will need ways to learn love and safe spaces to explore what love truly is. In fact, we may well need the love of God to correct some of our socially-informed (or misinformed) understandings of love, and we will need trustworthy ambassadors of that love in our own lives, as we learn what genuine love is.

Any process of genuine metanoia will need to integrate growth in our capacity to love, to be honest with one another, and to nurture the unique inner beauty and giftedness in ourselves and in others as part of the change that we and our world need. For metanoia, like falling in love, upends our lives, altering our perspectives and strengthening us to make profound changes that benefit the human community.

Love as the Fundamental Energy of Metanoia

When we look at the ways that people in the gospels experienced Jesus, receiving healing, consolation, empowerment and acceptance, we begin to understand the way of metanoia as a way of compassion and tenderness that is experienced with relief, joy, gratitude, and love. Theologian Albert Nolan offers us a helpful description of the depth of Jesus's compassion and how compassion and tenderness were expressions of his essence. He writes that compassion moves beyond a desire to be of assistance to the other, because it entails a participation in the experience of the other in order to be present and available in solidarity and communion. Compassion requires sensitivity to what is weak or wounded in the other, with a vulnerability that has us being moved by, affected by, and available to the other. Ultimately, compassion also demands action to alleviate pain and suffering in the other.

> English does not really have a word to describe this deep and visceral movement from the intestines, bowels, entrails or heart—that is, from the inward parts from which strong emotions seem to arise... a movement or impulse that wells up from one's very entrails... an eminently human feeling. (See Albert Nolan, *Jesus before Christianity*, p. 35)

We have already seen that a willingness to go beyond the self and a desire to learn from one another is an intrinsic part of the process of metanoia. Over time, this willingness fuels a desire to create new forms of community—communities of care that will not evolve when love is approached out of a sense of duty. A generosity of spirit is needed—one that infuses even the duties and legitimate demands of love with a quality that keeps our relationships from becoming transactional. The key ingredient still missing—the one that allows us to move from "hardness of heart"—one of the attitudes that seemed to most preoccupy Jesus—is the tenderness that allows empathy, connection, commitment, and joy.

> Tenderness is a learned habit, an acquired sensitivity born of solidarity and keen interest in the lives, challenges, struggles, and joys of others. We do not become tender because we want to, just like we do not become fit because we want to. Desire is important, but dedication is even more critical. We dedicate ourselves to growth in tenderness, just as we might to greater fitness or flexibility. (Ahlgren, *The Tenderness of God*, p. 74)

The most basic human point of reference for such tenderness is what we feel as we fall in love and nurture love in our lives.

Nothing is more practical than
finding God, that is, than
Falling in Love in a quite absolute, final way.
What you are in love with,
what seizes your imagination,
will affect everything.
It will decide
what will get you out of bed in the morning,
what you do with your evenings,
how you spend your weekends,
what you read, whom you know,
what breaks your heart,
and what amazes you with joy and gratitude.
Fall in love, stay in love,
and it will decide everything.

As the poem attributed to Pedro Arrupe suggests, falling in love and staying in love with the God who walks with us in the world does truly "change everything." We should be clear that our very identity is at stake as we walk together in a way of greater tenderness. As the faces of metanoia we explore in this volume make clear, our challenge as human beings is to embrace an evolving identity deeply informed by the ways that God reveals Godself to us, with and through the needs of others around us.

Change can be difficult, even as it can be exciting and liberating. Even though the changes involved in metanoia bring deeper possibility and fulfillment, they will still be a challenge, as Pope Francis noted:

Many things have to change course, but it is we human beings above all who need to change. We lack an awareness of our common origin, of our mutual belonging, and of a future to be shared with everyone. This basic awareness would enable the development of new convictions, attitudes and forms of life. A great cultural, spiritual and educational challenge stands before us, and it will demand that we set out on the long path of renewal. (Pope Francis, *On Care for Our Common Home*, par. 202)

It is important to remember that the changes involved in true metanoia are not implemented solely for ourselves or even by ourselves. For us, such changes (even if they are challenging) provide inherent benefits, drawing us out of malaise, complacency, confusion, and lack of fulfillment, and imparting meaning, fulfillment, and joy. It goes without question that the way of metanoia opens our eyes to the world around us: its beauty, the daily miracle of being alive, but also the cruelty and senselessness of much that passes for "normal." Metanoia sensitizes us to what is possible and emboldens us to be kinder, to risk revealing our own needs and vulnerabilities, and to appreciate the character and humanity of others. As the poem attributed to Pedro Arrupe reminds us, it is love that ultimately fuels metanoia and provides the courage and generosity that the invitation to deepening relationship with God needs. We learn and receive from God the love that empowers us to answer the call to change.

This education in love is what we learn from our four visionary leaders—Francis, Clare, Dorothy Day, and Oscar Romero— who provide faces and flesh to a word like metanoia, which may seem so abstract. They show us that a transforming relationship with God does not change only us; it changes the world around us. This dynamic is riveting, undeniable, and inspiring, enabling us to see that God's way is transformative, for them and for us. Radiating love was at the core of their imitation of Christ, and it is what makes their way of life special, even revolutionary. They oriented their lives toward the daily, direct communication of the life-giving love of God. This way of life responds directly to the question:

> For if we have received the love which restores meaning to our lives, how can we fail to share that love with others? (Pope Francis, *Joy of the Gospel*, par. 8)

Loving the God of life and love both invites and requires us to radiate love into a hurting world. And the visionary lives of Francis, Clare, Dorothy Day, and Oscar Romero give us viable models for how we, too, might love the world into greater life.

Moments of Metanoia
in Francis of Assisi

Most High, all glorious God,
enlighten the darkness of my heart.
Give me a right faith, certain hope, and perfect love,
with deep humility, wisdom and understanding,
that I may know and do Your most holy will.

- Prayer of Francis of Assisi

Early Life and the Unexpected Invitation

Francis of Assisi (c.1182-1226) was born into a society strongly divided by class—a society where walls strategically excluded people and demonstrated who mattered in society and who didn't. The topography of Assisi itself tells this vivid story: the noble class lived close to the fortress set high up on the hill, as far away as possible from the valley outside the city walls, where peasants, day workers, and others at the margins of society lived. Between those two groups, but still mostly within the city walls, lived the growing merchant class.

Francis' father Pietro di Bernardone was a powerful and influential man, although his status was constantly shadowed by the fact that he had acquired his wealth through the sale of luxury cloth, rather than having inherited his money, as a member of the noble class would have. He was a shrewd and ambitious businessman, and, as he acquired more and more wealth, he sought to purchase land in the valley below the city. In centuries past, feudal norms would have made such aspirations impossible. But times were changing. After years of drought and famine toward the end of the twelfth century, many noble families were willing to sell off tracts of land that no longer produced as much income as they needed.

By law, the merchant class was not allowed to own land, even if they had the money to purchase it. In 1198, when Francis was 16, Pietro helped finance an uprising of the merchant class in Assisi, who entered the noble section of the city, attacking and even occupying homes in an attempt to force changes in the laws regarding land ownership. Noble families fled first to the fortress above the city and then, when they were unable to take back their houses, they resettled to the local city of Perugia. Notably, Clare and her noble family were among these political refugees.

The rebellion of the merchant class could not go unanswered. Assisi's noble class forged an alliance with the Perugian nobles who had taken them in, extending what had begun as a struggle between two classes in Assisi to a small-scale civil war, as the Perugians attacked Assisi periodically over the next four years. In 1202, Francis, now 20, was too old to avoid being drafted into the defense of Assisi. He was wounded at a battle near the village of Collestrada, and the Perugians recognized by his armor that he was valuable enough to take back to Perugia as a prisoner of war. Francis was thrown into a prison cell until an appropriate ransom could be negotiated.

Most medieval people found life to be somewhat precarious. Diseases we can now treat fairly readily were fatal: diarrhea caused by food- or water-borne illness, infections from household accidents, even sexually-transmitted diseases could

Gillian T.W. Ahlgren

kill. For women, of course, daily life was even more dangerous, because childbirth could easily lead to death.

But Francis, from his privileged position prior to imprisonment, had been somewhat protected from the kinds of vulnerability routinely experienced by those who had no fixed meals, no comfortable bed, nothing to make daily life safe or easy. Dazed, in pain, and facing an uncertain future, Francis's year as a prisoner of war waiting to be ransomed back to his family gave him his first real taste of the grittiness of human existence. Some scholars have even suggested that he may have contracted malaria in captivity. We know from early biographers, that upon his return to Assisi in 1203, after a year of captivity, Francis was a changed person—psychologically and emotionally, not just physically. As he slowly started to piece his life back together, Francis had to wonder if anything was worth the sacrifice he and his generation had given.

Some scholars have referred to Francis' captivity and recovery as "the lost years," since we have very little concrete evidence about what war and captivity did to him. What I would like to suggest here is that Francis's time in Perugia, in particular, was ultimately an unexpected invitation for him to consider his life, his values, and whether or not he wanted to go back to "business as usual," as his father expected.

Part of the "aha moment" for him was that he now saw that owning property meant defending property, and he knew in his heart and his bones the cost of the violence of this. His recovery bed gave him plenty of time to wonder if fighting over property was really what God had in mind, for him and for the world. While he felt no attraction to his old way of life, he had no idea what, if anything, God was calling him toward.

"No one told me what I should do," he wrote in his Testament at the end of his life. The simplicity of Francis's statement suggests that what we today might see as a life of clarity and purpose evolved only gradually and in deepening dialogue with God. Francis now spent more time than ever in prayer. He sought out quiet places, in nature and in the abandoned church of San Damiano just outside the city walls. There he developed the prayer at the start of this chapter: a prayer for guidance and direction, a prayer of self-offering, the prayer of a simple spirit that anyone can pray.

FOR REFLECTION:

Francis's early life raises helpful points of reflection for us:

1. How have you experienced the pain and confusion of disruption in your life?

2. In that disruption have there been any unexpected invitations to change, growth or new perspectives?

3. In what ways have you ever felt hindered, either in your personal authenticity or in your relationship with God, by something in your personal or professional life?

4. Has honesty about how something is not working ever given you a way to grow toward something new?

5. Who are your conversation partners when you feel alone or confused?

6. What forms of prayer can provide deeper access to the God of your heart when you are troubled?

Eyes to See

God's invitation to Francis's next step was not long in coming. As he tells us unequivocally in his own account of "the way God had with me," Francis first learned the power of God in one of the most frightening spaces of the medieval world: a leper colony. How did he get there? What led Francis to venture out into the space of the outcast?

We last saw Francis grappling with a growing awareness of his human vulnerability and with many questions about the values he had inherited from his family and his society. His return to Assisi, while a liberation from the hardships of confinement in the prison of Perugia, was not easy. Medieval people lacked our contemporary psychological and medical understanding of post-combat trauma, but that lens helps us to imagine even more holistically the crisis of meaning Francis experienced after war and imprisonment. Perhaps an integral part of the "long illness" that then ate at him was the challenge of reflecting on the worth and value of his life up to this point and feeling that he had done nothing that was lasting, meaningful or significant. "Is this really all there is?" Forced, first in the prison cell in Perugia and then on the sickbed in Assisi, to try to make peace with his heart, perhaps Francis intuitively sensed that following his discontent to its roots and seeking remedy and guidance from God from that space of vulnerability was not only possible but might be the only way to true happiness.

In his Testament, Francis suggests that being drawn into the leper colony and the flood of feelings that overcame him once there was, for him, a singular expression of God's compassionate and tender love. Although we can and should speak of this experience as Francis's first knowledge of God's radical tenderness, it was not solely a sentimental experience, nor even an immediate denouement in the drama of his life. Francis's first experience of his sisters and brothers in the leper community did, however, suspend his malaise and despair by providing him a depth of connection to sisters and brothers abandoned to disease and death. Through it, he felt a quickening of life flowing through him that empowered him toward commitment to and solidarity with people who had always horrified him. All of this showed Francis instantly and directly both who God was and who God called him to be.

Outside the city walls of Assisi there were several leper colonies: spaces that people, including Francis, carefully avoided. Francis's first real encounter with lepers in 1206 was hardly the first time he became aware of them. Leprosy was probably the most feared condition in medieval Europe: the disease ravaged human bodies and gradually left people unable to walk, bathe, or feed themselves. In addition to being untreatable, leprosy was considered immediately contagious. Contact with lepers was strictly forbidden, and city statutes kept lepers from ever entering the city walls. Any leper who violated these prohibitions could be beaten with impunity, according to medieval law.

Leprosy was a wretched and painful condition, but the suffering that lepers endured was more than simply physical. It was emotional, relational, and social. Lepers could not work, nor could they maintain contact with their families. Such restrictions rendered them helpless long before their disease ran its course and absorbed any identity beyond that of "leper" that they might ever have had. As lepers, their clothing, begging bowl, clapper, and warning bell set them apart from the world, and the leper colony was a place of extreme deprivation, even unto death. No self-respecting person in Francis's society could or would associate with these untouchables; to enter a leper colony was like stepping across a threshold into the netherworld.

Francis could never have predicted that he would find God among the lepers. But from his first visit, he knew that something radical had happened within him, and he knew that

Gillian T.W. Ahlgren

from the wellspring of tenderness that erupted inside him—a tenderness he knew that he himself was not capable of. He understood this, immediately, as the love of God, drawing him to love others. It was a life-changing moment that set in motion all of the next steps of his life. "What had once been bitter to me," he tells us, "now seemed sweet." The stunning experience of finding God in what was, for Francis, the most unexpected and unimaginable place—a place of horror and suffering—must have been profoundly disconcerting. And yet to have found love, connection, passion, and even joy in a place that he expected to feel disgust was also compelling.

This significant moment of metanoia, mediated through life-changing encounter with those with nowhere to go, gave Francis eyes to see—to see the world from a perspective informed by gratuitous and unnecessary suffering, to see the world the way God sees it, to see the world as a space where Love seeks to console, strengthen, encourage, and transform.

> The Gospel tells us constantly to run the risk of a face-to-face encounter with others, with their physical presence which challenges us, with their pain and their pleas, with their joy which infects us in our close and continuous interaction. In becoming flesh, God, in Christ, summons us to the revolution of tenderness. (Pope Francis, *Joy of the Gospel*)

What does this "revolution of tenderness" look like? Where might we even start? Francis felt the same wonder, curiosity, and concern that we might feel as we contemplate such questions. As he left the leper colony for the first time, Francis had to be wondering where "home" really was, for him. The lepers had given him access to something new: access to the presence and love of God, access to his own heart… access to things that he could not find in the world around him inside the comfort of the city walls. For as he now saw, both from his knowledge of the cost of war and from the life of the discarded, that comfort was built on the backs of others.

As Francis began to accept vulnerability as an integral element of his own humanity, he found he had much to learn from those who lived with the pain of feeling rejected, ignored, and alone. For several years he had known that something profound was missing from his life: now the joy and fellowship he found with those left for dead gave him a new clue as to how to find meaning in his own life. Francis's initial experience at the leper colony validated his growing instinct to question his life, its meaning, and the goals that his family and society imposed upon him. The hollowness of all that he had, to this point, willingly and even anxiously embraced was exposed for what it was: a heartlessness that could never fulfill or even satisfy.

By this point in his post-war recovery, Francis had already discovered the abandoned church of San Damiano, a place where prayer seemed to come a bit more easily to him. Spending more time there, the desire to rebuild it, stone by stone, overcame him, and he began to commit himself to that project, despite the fact that he knew his father would not approve. He began to inhabit an intermediate, almost liminal, space in which he had the freedom to realize that he was, as I have written before, just as homeless as the lepers who had shown him his own heart and had given him access to the very heart of God. The more that he considered this somewhat shocking mystery, the more Francis sensed that down in the exposed plain of the valley, amidst those with nowhere else to go, he had finally found home. And a new and ultimate purpose for his life: to work with others to make the world a home for all.

This revelation, which would gradually become a "revolution of tenderness" as Pope Francis identifies the invitation of Jesus above, hinged around a basic, yet central question rooted in the gospels: What do we learn from the richness of our shared

Gillian T.W. Ahlgren

humanity, as we work together to ensure that all have the love and care that we need in order to flourish?

Francis and Clare were unafraid to accept vulnerability as a source of commonality, even of communion. They open a way for us today to find the courage to turn away from what is not working, to understand ourselves as sisters and brothers to all, and to commit the vitality and creativity that emerges as we journey together to become a community of belonging and solidarity worthy of our time, our energy and our resources despite the challenges ahead. (Ahlgren, *The Tenderness of God*)

FOR REFLECTION:

Francis's simplicity, humility and joy gradually provided deep spiritual grounding for living with integrity and purity of heart. In the spirit of Francis, we might ask:

1.   Can we ask for the grace to weep over our indifference, to weep over the cruelty of our world, to lament the ways that so many of us make social and economic decisions which close our minds and hearts to what is possible if we lived in solidarity and collaboration?

2.   How can our vulnerability and the commonality of our suffering become a deeper source of solidarity and change?

3.   What have you learned that you can learn only at the margins?

Radical Departure/Beyond Barriers

In Francis's life, the next moment of metanoia is one of decisive action. Everything that preceded this moment had been leading up to it, for there was only so much that his father, his friends and family, and the social and cultural norms in which he lived would tolerate. Many of us already know about the drama of the moment when Francis stripped himself naked before Bishop Guido of Assisi, but it is worth our time to review what led up to it, and what lies at the core and heart of this moment.

Looking at Francis's journey so far from the vantage point of Pietro di Bernardone, Francis's father, we might not judge so harshly his increasing frustration with his eldest son. Before his apprenticeship in the family business had been interrupted by the war with Perugia, Francis had been a carefree and popular young man, known about Assisi for his charm, wit, humor, and kindness. His father indulged Francis's gregarious nature, especially because every time Francis hosted a party or social gathering, everyone in the city could see that the Bernardones were a family that mattered. At the same time, by the age of fifteen, when Francis could consciously enter a period of apprenticeship, his father invested a lot of time carefully teaching him the logistics of the family business, from identifying and selling the silk fabrics and brocades that would attract the attention of the nobility to how to invest the family profits.

The plan had always been that Francis would be as aggressive a businessman as Pietro, a man who could not relate to Francis's sensitivities and had no patience for Francis's crisis of meaning. Pietro worried that Francis's illness threatened the stability of the family fortune, into which Pietro had devoted his lifeblood. As he slowly realized that Francis had no intention of pursuing profit, Pietro filed a complaint with the civil courts, requesting a hearing to have Francis punished for using some of the family's money for the reconstruction of the church of San Damiano and for refusing to shoulder the responsibilities for the family's professional standing and financial well-being.

There was a civil protocol for this; in order to protect the family fortune, parents could have their adult children banished from the city on the grounds of parental disobedience. Pietro's case came before the civil judge in early 1207, and, when a messenger arrived at San Damiano to serve Francis with his summons, Francis claimed he was exempt from civil law because, as he saw things, he was now working in the service of the church. The consuls referred Pietro to the bishop. Biographical and historical sources converge on this dramatic event: pleading his case before Bishop Guido outside the bishop's residence, Pietro demanded the return of the money from the sale of cloth and the horse in Foligno. In response, Francis not only gave it to him, but stripped himself of his fine clothing, standing naked before all and handing everything back to his father. In one fell blow, he had renounced his inheritance, his status in society, and his identity as the son of Pietro di Bernardone. By saying no to the social and economic forces he felt were choking him, Francis could discover, with God, what might come next.

How are we today to understand this moment of metanoia? We could start be recognizing it as both a deeply spiritual and a deeply human act—a holistic decision involving the whole of his personhood, in an action that was both personal and relational. It was Francis's humanity that was being compromised by the political, economic, social, and religious structures of his time. And, as he fully recognized, those structures compromised others as much as they compromised him. There had to be a better way.

It was perfectly legitimate, in Francis's day, for people (including churchgoing Christians) to display contempt toward those who lived in the leper colony, begged for a living, or otherwise lived in the margins of society. In understanding the cost of such contempt for others to his humanity (not just his spiritual integrity), Francis was making a compelling case for our need, then and now, to free ourselves from anything that debases any and all of us. I think of this as a statement of personal integrity as well as a prophetic statement to the whole human community, almost like saying: "Our way of life so compromises my integrity that I must divest myself from it. I may not know exactly who I am being called to become, but I do know that I cannot become who I must without setting off upon an entirely different way." Francis's departure from his family, his social class, and the many ways that his life was being determined for him was an act of fidelity to the God who was inviting Francis to a simple way of justice, humility, solidarity, and tenderness.

I have called this third moment of metanoia in Francis "Radical Departure/Beyond Barriers" because of the stark choice he made to live outside the city walls. As we have seen, this decision caused a rupture with his father—a public scene before the bishop of Assisi in which Francis renounced any claim to inheritance—and a departure from social structures in order to live according to the gospels—to eat, like Jesus, with anyone, including the unclean, and to live with those with nowhere safe to live. Gradually this gospel-informed way of life—one in which poverty as a form of solidarity and as an experiment in grace guided communal life—attracted others, slowly growing into a major revolution in religious life.

FOR REFLECTION:

1. Francis's example shows us that a life of fidelity and integrity cannot be built on a fundamentally flawed foundation: space must be cleared for freedom of spirit and growth toward a genuine, adult partnership with God. Based on what you now know about

Francis's life, list and describe some of the things he would say no to in today's world. Why would he say no to them?

2. What greater clarity does Francis's "no" give to you to turn away from some of our own cultural and social norms?

3. If saying "no" to some things creates more space to say "yes" to God, where and how can you clear greater space for the work of God in your life and in the world around you?

Radiating Love

We return to Francis's Testament and its stark commentary: "No one told me what I should do..." only to find the text continuing, "...But then God gave me brothers." To his surprise, Francis's sincerity and the simplicity of his life rebuilding churches in the valley, tending to those in the leper communities, and working alongside day laborers, quickly began attracting others willing to give up their wealth and social position, just as Francis had. One of the earliest of these was a wealthy, educated nobleman named Bernardo di Quintavalle, whose dedication to poverty must have caused as much public scandal as Francis's had. Bernardo had degrees in both civil and canon law and was much respected around the city. After consulting with Francis, he liquidated his extensive assets, including tracts of land on the hill and in the valley below Assisi, with their olive groves and vineyards. All the proceeds were given away to the poor. Joined by another doctor of law, Peter of Catania, and one of Clare's own cousins, Rufino, the group settled into the Portiuncula down in the valley, another church that they were restoring.

By the fall of 1209, when Francis and his companions numbered eight, they decided to leave Assisi on a lengthy preaching tour; according to Thomas of Celano, two of them went as far as Santiago de Compostela in northwestern Spain. Francis was living his dream of the gospel life, practicing as precise an imitation of Christ as he knew. But leaving the confines and jurisdiction of the Spoleto valley required more ecclesiastical support than the bishop of Assisi could grant. As Francis's revolutionary way of life began to catch on, it attracted attention, notoriety, and the possibility of resistance.

Because Francis wanted the freedom both to preach and to invite others into this gospel life, in 1209 or 1210, he wrote out a simple way of life, and went with his brothers down to Rome to seek papal approval of this new way. Pope Innocent III's verbal approval of this way led to two significant developments. First, the brothers could expand as a religious community, and, second, they could now figure out how to formally incorporate the noblewoman Clare, who had supported their work since she had first learned of it through her cousin Rufino. We will look extensively at Clare's journey and her role in the movement in the next chapter. What remains for us to do, as we explore this longer moment of metanoia, is to consider the principles for living that Francis and the earliest communities were putting into practice.

What Francis wanted to re-capture and live was what the earliest companions of Jesus had experienced: the presence of God coming alive in the human community. He wanted that to be the universal Christian way. Francis saw the living God in the discarded, and he wanted everyone else to see God there, too. He understood the forces that he and his contemporaries were up against. He had seen how his own neighbors closed their eyes to the suffering poor, discarded those who were unproductive, and then built walls to protect their consciences from seeing what they had done. But he had also been shown that he could, in some small way, remediate human indifference and exploitation by radiating love and the tender care that cherished those that society deemed worthless. Francis saw all of this simply. He was interested in establishing a home for God in the human community—a place that Jesus would recognize because it welcomed the stranger, fed the hungry and clothed the naked. He wanted everyone to pursue a shared desire and a shared commitment to find Christ incarnate in our midst, without walls and without exclusion, and he did not think that any endeavor short of that was particularly Christian.

As Francis and his companions walked back to Assisi from Rome, contemplating their new status within the church at large, they asked themselves how they could best be living examples of the gospel. They had already given away what they had in joining the community. Now they committed themselves, as individuals and as a community, to the daily precariousness of the poor and homeless by begging each day for the food they needed to sustain themselves. They also committed to preaching the reign of God—that is, to describing the teachings and practices of Jesus as a way of life open to all. But they captured Jesus's way of life in ways that were not theoretical or abstract but full of tenderness and concern, uplifting all who felt trampled down. Their consistent presence in leper colonies, feeding and bathing those unable to care for themselves and tending to wounds taught and demonstrated how God's love always seeks, desires, and protects the good of others.

Both Francis and Clare, as she later developed a way of life for the Poor Ladies, modeled a way of life that rejects whatever diminishes or devalues the holiness of each human encounter, and in that way they model for us how to say "no" to the many forces in our world that threaten life and dignity. As the drama of their initial conversion gives way to the larger context of forming life-giving communities of care, hope and vision, they help us see how our deepening conversion to solidarity creates a space for God to come alive more fully in our own world. For Francis and Clare, radical poverty (saying "no" to all that dehumanizes us) is concurrently a way to make more space for the indwelling presence of God in our communities.

From early on, Francis and Clare's "new way" was a complete immersion into the gospel life, to live as Jesus and his companions had. But how to actually nurture a dedicated and life-giving communal relationship with God that would provide inner light and direction for daily life was something that needed to be learned. If we are to understand what was truly revolutionary about Francis and Clare's way of embodying the gospel life, we must identify the core spiritual values that, together, support a love that gives life and helps us continue to grow toward what is noble, right, pure, lovely, admirable, and excellent. (See Philippians 4:8) And we will have to learn and integrate into our daily life a liberating, humanizing, uplifting kind of love, for it may be that some of us have never actually experienced that.

Over and over, in both the Hebrew and Christian scriptures, love is defined for us by God—a God whose tender regard for humanity teaches us about what matters in life. The prophet Micah states clearly that all God requires of us is three things: to act justly, to love tenderly, and to walk humbly with our God. (Micah 6:8) And Jesus, citing the Deuteronomic tradition, tells us that our one responsibility is: "You shall love the Lord your God with all your heart, all your soul, and all your strength and love your neighbor as yourself." (See Deuteronomy 6:5, Mark 12:28-31, Matthew 22: 36-40, Luke 10:27.) These basic principles of reverence, justice, and collaboration can move us toward the universal solidarity that we and our world need.

Dedicating ourselves, inside and outside our communities of faith, to shared encounters with the God who lives in each one of us can help us discover and create together new ways of living sustainably and as a single human family. Pope Francis spoke often about building "a culture of encounter" and stated clearly that, in order to do so, we would need to employ "a language of generous, relational and existential love that touches the heart, impacts life, and awakens hope and desires." (See Pope Francis, *Christ is Alive*, par. 211.) To "speak" this way is not so much to use words but to be there for others and to move beyond our own limitations to live with integrity. In other words, the famous phrase associated with Francis, "Preach the gospel at all times; use words when necessary" is suggestive of a love that radiates out of us because it is centered and grounded in the God of love. Both Francis and Clare show us that we, too, can embody the truth of 1 John 4:16: "God is love. Whoever lives in love, lives in God, and God lives in them." The more that we are drawn into this love and come to know God, the more that we desire to be instruments of that love.

We also know that, for love to grow, it must be rooted in a community oriented to cultivating and nurturing the growth of all of its members. We have already seen elements of the kind of growth we are talking about: growth in integrity, in maturity, in wisdom, courage, honesty, solidarity and love. If no single quality can capture God's tenderness, we can certainly understand it as the antonym to hard-heartedness.

In most of our world today, tenderness is counter-cultural. Few of us are taught tenderness as a quality to be valued or grown. For us today, we grow into deeper tenderness as we embrace tenderness not as a quality only a few people were born with, but as a learned habit, an acquired sensitivity born of solidarity and keen interest in the lives, challenges, struggles, and joys of others. When we really listen to the stories and struggles and hopes of others, and when we spend enough time in the solitude of our own hearts, we can begin the journey to tenderness that will imbue life with greater meaning and greater joy.

Francis's way of life was intended to be a direct communication of the life-giving love of God—a transforming love that we receive and seek to share with others. His tender care of others allowed them to see love in concrete, practical action: encouraging, supporting, sustaining, protecting, cherishing, even admonishing where necessary. Both Francis and Clare illuminated the truth of love's power by showing what love does, how love behaves, and what the generosity of spirit that flows out of a heart full of love looks like. As others saw the possibility of life-giving love, they, too, wanted to experience its transformative impact and radiate it into the world around them.

Three elements characterize the emerging Franciscan model of community: (1) active care for one another; (2) solidarity, equality, and invested relationship with others; and (3) prophetic resistance to injustice and sin. Francis and Clare embodied the gospel's invitation to engage our human interrelatedness, our responsibility to one another, and the holiness that being human involves. This is, first and foremost, a human journey, one of universal solidarity, in which the "slow and arduous effort" of becoming a people requires "integration and a willingness to achieve this through the growth of a peaceful and multifaceted culture of encounter." (Pope Francis, *Joy of the Gospel*, par. 220; see also Pope Francis, **Laudato Si': On Care for Our Common Home**, par. 14.) Ultimately, cultivating tender care for one another leads to new forms of life-enhancing love which benefit all of us, individually and collectively.

In conclusion we note that the way of Francis and Clare was a way of life-giving love that prioritizes a relational experience of personhood over an egocentric one, with an intentional desire to affirm, support, and enhance the presence of God in our midst. Francis and Clare exemplified the power of God's own tenderness by translating what they had learned about God's love into a way of being in human community. The earliest communities, at San Damiano and the Portiuncula, were living schools, training people in the daily practice of loving solidarity, as this was modeled by Christ. The assumption in those communities was that all would be continually growing in the tenderness and loving kindness that protects, sustains, and supports the presence of God in the human community. What would that look like in today's world?

FOR REFLECTION:

1. Consider some of the relationships that shape your personal or professional life. How would or might an approach of greater tenderness change one of them?

2. In what spaces and under what conditions do you feel most able to engage your deepest emotions and share them fruitfully with others? How might you cultivate tenderness?

3. What do we lose when we lose our tenderness and our capacity to be moved?

The Revolution of Tenderness

The fifth stage of metanoia in Francis's life has to do with both the ways that life-giving love changed the world around him but also, and more importantly, with the seeds that he sowed to ensure that the way of tenderness would not be lost over time. Francis knew that he would not live forever. As his order expanded, and some of the newcomers questioned both his principles of radical simplicity and radical love at the margins of society, Francis had to think hard and fast about how to communicate, in a lasting way, the lessons about life and love that he understood God to have taught him.

Francis's final years were some of his fullest and most impressive. In 1219 he met with the Ayyubid Sultan Malik al-Kamil in Damietta, Egypt in the midst of the Fifth Crusade. Whether Francis originally sought martyrdom or peacemaking is less clear than that his meeting with the Sultan was effectively the first inter-religious dialogue in the midst of religious conflict that we know about. The exchange left both men changed, and the ivory horn that the Sultan gave Francis as a safe-conduct for his return to Italy (usually housed in the lower basilica of St. Francis in the same chapel where Francis's habit is displayed) remains a cherished memento of the occasion. Francis set out on the long journey home, and at this point, may have contracted the eye infection that plagued him for the rest of his life.

As Franciscan communities grew and expanded in Europe, Francis himself turned more deeply inward, turning administration of the order over to others and dedicating himself even more deeply to prayer. In August 1224, wanting to be sure that he had been as faithful as possible to the gifts and insights God had given him, Francis went to La Verna to engage an extended retreat and received the stigmata. Suffering from both the eyes and now wounds on his body, Francis sought treatment and spent time at San Damiano, where he consulted with Clare and in 1225 wrote the Canticle of Creation, his hymn of praise and thanksgiving to God for the goodness of creation. Francis called the sun, the moon, the natural elements and even death, "sisters" and "brothers," accentuating the union of all things in God. As Francis sought deepening intimacy with God in his own life, he modeled a commitment to mystical growth that Clare and others would carry into subsequent decades. Francis's dying impulse was to continue inviting people into a collaborative partnership with God that changes the lives of others and makes for a kinder, better world.

Gillian T.W. Ahlgren

FOR REFLECTION:

1. How are we today engaging a revolution of tenderness that can inspire others?

2. How are we engaging with others in the work of making this world a home for all?

3. Are you intentional about the legacy of love that you are creating in the world around you? If so, how can you intensify your efforts? If not, how do you want to be remembered, and what do you want to leave in the world around you when you are gone?

Moments of Metanoia
in Clare of Assisi

Place your mind before the mirror of eternity!
Place your soul in the brilliance of glory!
Place your heart in the figure of the divine substance
and, through contemplation,
transform your entire being into the image
of the Godhead itself,
So that you too may feel what friends feel
in tasting the hidden sweetness
that, from the beginning,
God has reserved for all who love God.

- Clare's Third Letter to Agnes of Prague (c. 1238)

The Unexpected Invitation and the Radical Departure/ Beyond Barriers

As we turn to Clare of Assisi (c.1193-1253) to explore her journey toward a flourishing partnership with God, we can use the same five stages of metanoia as we examined in Francis's life, but we will see how the order and sequence of them varies a bit. As a woman, Clare faced all of the challenges of parental and social expectation that Francis did; however, those expectations cut into her life even more deeply, impacting when and whom she would marry and keeping her from ordering her life around her desire for God. In many ways, Clare was not really waiting for God to invite her toward deepening relationship. Clare was actively seeking how to be faithful to the call of the gospel and to the crucified One in ways that her culture did not allow women to pursue.

Clare came from one of the most powerful noble families in Assisi; their palatial home abutted the ancient church of San Rufino and looked out over a beautiful piazza. Clare was 4 or 5 years old in 1198, when the uprising of Assisi's merchant class displaced her family from their home. She and her mother and sisters became political refugees, living in neighboring Perugia for nearly eight years, while the men in the family participated in the war to gain back their homes and positions in Assisi. When the family returned to Assisi eight or nine years later, Clare had reached the age of betrothal, but she showed more interest in the activities of Francis down in the valley than in marrying someone her family chose for her.

Like everyone in Assisi, Clare knew about Francis's dramatic renunciation of his inheritance and family name. But because her cousin Rufino had joined Francis and worked beside him, rebuilding churches and ministering in the leper colonies around Assisi, Clare knew more than most about his new movement and its ideals. Francis's sincerity and simplicity attracted her, and she became an early financial supporter of his work, sending the brothers money from the household budget and even from her dowry. Her childhood friend Bona of Guelfuccio later testified that Clare had given her money to take down to "those who were working on Saint Mary of the Portiuncula" so that they had food and provisions for the rebuilding of the church, confirming Clare's active collaboration with Francis as early as 1208 or 1209.

For most women, there would have been no possibility of closer connection than as something of a patron. But Clare was not

Gillian T.W. Ahlgren

most women. She had a reputation around Assisi for goodness, even holiness, always aspiring to kindness, compassion, and purity of heart. Francis came to know more about Clare, and they had a mutual interest in and admiration for one another. They met to speak with one another, and, as soon as Francis's way of life was approved by Pope Innocent III, they developed a plan for Clare to join the community as its first woman in a move no less dramatic than Francis's own start in religious life.

Clare's attraction to the gospel call was, in fact, far more predictable than Francis's—not really an "unexpected invitation" at all. What Clare needed was a path and an ally to support her radical commitment to God. In Francis she found a true companion. But both of them knew that Clare's family would never tolerate a divergence from the marriage they had already arranged. In the medieval period, such marriages were critical to sustaining the financial stability of noble families.

Francis and Clare concocted Clare's escape plan in secret, with the approval of the local bishop, Guido, who had already supported Francis in his dispute with his father. Late at night, while everyone in her household was asleep, Clare slipped out of her home, passed through the city walls, and headed down to the church of the Portiuncula, where Francis and his brothers waited for her. Francis received her vows to religious life and sealed her consecration to God by cutting off her long and lovely hair. Clare had realized her dream to pursue religious life and could now live out her vocation.

But she could not stay at the Portiuncula. Instead, Clare and Francis walked about four kilometers, before dawn, to the Benedictine convent of San Paolo delle Abadesse. As everyone in the valley below Assisi knew, this convent had a special privilege, granted by Pope Innocent III himself, to provide safety to women seeking refuge and asylum. When we remember the vulnerability of those living in the valley between Assisi and Perugia, which had been the central battlefield during the longstanding civil war, we can understand why such a papal privilege might have been necessary.

Francis and Clare's choice of San Paolo delle Abadesse for Clare could not have been casual or uninformed. In fact, it was an astute decision, meant to protect Clare from the resistance they predicted she would face from her family. Even if they went out searching for her after her disappearance, under church law, the men in Clare's family could not disrupt the functioning of the convent, and they certainly could not enter with an intent to violence. It was both telling and shocking when, the very next morning, a posse of male relatives arrived at the convent door and stormed into the community's church demanding Clare's return and prepared to seize her by force, if necessary.

In a dramatic show of courage and conviction, Clare stood before the altar of the church and removed her veil, showing her shorn head, the symbol of her consecration to God. Her male relatives were too late: having taken religious vows, she could and would no longer marry. The men left, confused, thrown off guard, and frustrated. Like Francis as soon as he had stripped himself before the bishop, Clare, too, was now free.

FOR REFLECTION:

1. In what ways have you renounced something that might have kept you from furthering your relationship with God?

2. Who are your allies in pursuing goodness and deepening your commitment to God?

3. In your journey toward personal integrity and self-

realization, what resistance have you encountered, and how have you overcome that resistance?

Eyes to See

While Clare did not seem to need those at the margins giving her eyes to see what they suffered, her struggles and those of her sister Catherine can give us eyes to see how, at times, there are forces at work actively attempting to disable our collaboration with God and the radical courage that it took for women to pursue a life of partnership with God.

Clare's stay at San Paolo delle Abbadesse did not last long. While the Benedictine nuns there had taken the traditional vows of poverty, chastity and obedience, they lived in relative comfort. From Clare's perspective, the community's large endowment kept the nuns from experiencing genuine poverty, particularly in the form of deprivation or precarity, like most people who lived outside the city walls. Once she knew she was safe from the vengeance of her family and no longer needed the protection of the convent's papal privilege, Clare transferred herself to a small community called Sant'Angelo in Panzo, where women from poorer families were gathered. These women lacked the dowry to join more formal convents, but, like many medieval women, wanted to support one another's spiritual growth in community. Here Clare could live in a way that she felt was more consistent with the simplicity of life captured in Francis's reform movement.

Clare had not been at Sant'Angelo in Panzo for long when, to her surprise, her sister Catherine appeared. Inspired by Clare's decision and determined to join her in religious life, Catherine, too, had decided to run away from the family home, seeking an alternate way of life. But this unexpected turn of events caught both Clare and Francis off guard. Francis was not on hand to receive Catherine's vows, and Clare did not have the privilege of the Benedictine community to protect her when her male relatives showed up to haul Catherine back home. The protests of the women did little to counter the men's violence against Catherine. Throwing her to the ground they tried to beat her into submission. According to the legend tradition, Catherine's body "grew as heavy as lead," and the men were unable to drag her back to the family palace. It is just as likely that the silent testimony of Catherine's torn clothing and bloodied body kept the Offreduccio knights from taking Catherine back through the streets of Assisi. Instead, they left her with Clare, perhaps thinking that she was already dead. Clare's solicitous care combined with her knowledge of herbal medicines helped Catherine heal from the assault. When Francis arrived to receive Catherine's vows, he suggested that Catherine take the name Agnes for her name in religious life, after the early Christian martyr, since her path to religious life had cost her so much.

It was not much longer before the dormitory that Francis and the brothers had been adding to the church of San Damiano was ready for Clare and Catherine to live in. Safely housed there, Clare could begin to grow the community of Poor Ladies and pray about how the women could best live out their spiritual ideals. Eventually Clare wrote a more formal Way of Life for the Poor Ladies. These communities eventually spread beyond Italy, bolstered by a new convent of Poor Ladies founded by Agnes of Prague, from the Bohemian royal family. Inspired by the model of Clare, which Agnes learned about from Franciscan brothers, Agnes chose the life of poverty over royal marriage. Wanting to Support Agnes's decision and provide whatever spiritual counsel she might need, Clare's correspondence with Agnes constitutes a noteworthy and beautiful contribution to Christian spirituality, providing us with many insights into Clare's method of prayer, "Gaze, Consider, Contemplate, Imitate." We will explore that method below, as we consider how, from the space of San Damiano, Clare moved beyond barriers to radiate love of God into the world.

FOR REFLECTION:

Both Clare and Francis's lives teach us the importance of saying "No" to whatever hinders our relationship with God, so that we can say a full and complete "yes" to growing collaboration with God in our lives. Consider the following, from *The Tenderness of God: Reclaiming Our Humanity*:

- For love to grow, it must be rooted and grounded in a community oriented to cultivating and nurturing the growth of all its members.

- Human life is meant to be deeply relational, best lived in solidarity and communion with one another and with God.

- We have the capacity to share life-giving love. This is the good news: that we can learn love, from God and from one another, as we share life together in graced encounter.

- Creating a dwelling place for God, a suitable home—in our hearts, our communities, and our world—for the One whose love gives life, is at the very core of the Gospel way.

What has your own experience of life taught you about the above statements, and do they ring true in your experience? How have you grown your own capacity to love?

Radiating Love

We cannot radiate love into the human community if we are not already filled with the love of God through the constancy of our connection with God. When you read Clare's words of counsel to Agnes of Prague, contained in the four extant letters Clare wrote to Agnes between 1234 and 1253, you glimpse the soul of a woman whose wisdom and kindness seems transcendent—someone with deep experiential knowledge of God's love. Clare's letters are studded with reference to scripture, especially the nuptial imagery of the Song of Songs, reflecting Clare's knowledge that she is richly loved by God. Their prayerful tone celebrates life and provides pearls of wisdom about God's kindness to all who read them.

Not all monastic correspondence is as effusive and uplifting as Clare's four letters to Agnes, but Clare's letters fit into a genre of literature that women in particular excelled at. Hildegard of Bingen, Catherine of Siena, Teresa of Avila, and many other visionary women all used this form to personalize and make real the mystical life that they aspired to—teaching through these letters in ways that most of them could not through the pulpit. We should remember that such letters, even when addressed to a single person, like Clare's to Agnes, were not personal. They would be read aloud in community, so that all could benefit from their wisdom. Clare derived this wisdom from her direct and continual contact with God in prayer. Over time, from the moment of her self-consecration, her life became an extended prayer that daily grew more loving and mature.

The model of living that Clare embodies is one of overflow: we drink from the well of love that is God, and that love spills out into the community around us. To approach this model, we must dedicate time and energy to the continual cultivation of our connection with God. Clare calls this process contemplation, and she outlines four facets to the contemplative process. Before we consider the four facets, we should first define contemplation in a way that makes it approachable to all of us.

When I present Clare's contemplative insights in workshops or retreats, I typically begin with a simple question: "How many of you consider yourself contemplative?" It's amazing how a room that, up to this point, has housed boisterous and enthusiastic conversation quickly grows silent. People look around the circle, as two or three brave souls hesitantly raise their hands, as if contemplation connotes a particular temperament. But, like many teachers of contemplation, Clare would want us to think of contemplation as an expression of love—an expression that grows more intelligent, patient, and tenacious because it proceeds from the knowledge that we are loved and a deepening awareness of Who it is who loves us. This fundamental definition of contemplation allows us to appreciate that contemplation is a practical, living, empowering, transforming way of life that supports and energizes us at all levels of our being.

Another way to think of contemplation is to consider it as encompassing the many ways that we grow in relationship with God. That is to say, as we bring the whole of our lives into growing dialogue with God, through prayer, reflection, and conversations about the meaning and purpose of our lives (including our worries, concerns, hopes, and dreams) and, fundamentally, as we listen and take in all that God has to say to us, we are engaging the contemplative life.

To summarize some of the insights about contemplation that we can glean from Clare's life, consider the following:

- Contemplation is, first and foremost, a disposition, a willingness to engage a process, to change and be changed.

- Contemplation is an invitation to experience the God who

is at the center of our being and who walks with us out of the margins of our own existence.

- Contemplation means growth in integrity, in maturity, in wisdom, courage, honesty, solidarity, and love.

- Contemplation and prayer give us eyes to see the world and others around us from a space of loving connection.

- A contemplative person is one who never stops asking "what is real?"

- Contemplation is less about leaving the world and more about becoming real. As more of us dedicate ourselves to the process of becoming authentically ourselves and sharing our giftedness with others, the world becomes a different place.

- Contemplation is not an individual process but a relational one: it is an integral part of the process of falling in love with the One whose love is beyond all telling. No one can fully embrace a relationship with God without contemplation. Engaging more deeply in our relationship with God is inherently transformative, helping us to reshape our priorities, values, daily practices, and capacity to see ourselves and our world anew.

- The converted, contemplative person values and lives toward simplicity, integrity, and relational honesty.

- Contemplation manifests itself in courage, calm, warmth, and vitality as our inner access to radical love radiates outward.

- A contemplative community brings wisdom, discretion, inspiration, and visionary leadership into the world. Like

Jesus and his earliest companions, such a community nurtures growth and calls us to be accountable to the impulses that stir us toward the common good.

- Contemplation is the grounding for us to learn how to collaborate with the divine in every facet of our lives.

- Contemplation is the space in which we learn not only God's aliveness but God's desire to make us partners with God in the work of making the world a better place. In this sense, there is no real tension between contemplation and action. The contemplative life moves toward prophetic action, and the active life craves the contemplative grounding that is so necessary for apostolic witness.

Does this functional definition make contemplation more attractive? If so, a development of Clare's four-fold method of prayer will make contemplation more accessible to you, whoever you are and whatever your temperament and prayer style. (And for a deeper introduction to contemplation, please see chapter five of *The Tenderness of God*, which is dedicated to this material.)

Clare's Method of Prayer:
Gaze, Consider, Contemplate, Imitate

GAZE: We start with the practice of the gaze, a very simple practice that all of us can do. To gaze is to look lovingly at another or at the world. To behold rather than to scrutinize and examine. We can gaze upon another person or a group of people, out into nature, or even upon a situation. We cultivate a holistic relationship with what we see by beholding with reverent attention and tenderness of heart. Gazing entails a particular (loving) attitude, disposition, and presence in us. This more open stance predisposes us to learn from what we see, to be transformed by what we take in.

CONSIDER: Consideration brings reflection into the relationship begun by the gaze. Consideration integrates the intellect with the heart from a loving space of greater, focused attention. Consideration refines the gaze by centering it in a space of single-mindedness, allowing us to wonder, inquire about and explore what we see in ways that respect and honor the other. Considering allows us to enter into the reality of the other, so that our own perspectives are enhanced and enriched.

CONTEMPLATE: Contemplation invites the divine into our lives and our relationships. It opens a space for us to ask God about what we are seeing and to bring God into how we engage with the world around us. Contemplation is the awareness, consent to, and participation in the aliveness of God. Contemplation is the relational grounding for us to learn how to collaborate with the divine in every aspect of our lives. Contemplation thrives in quiet, but it is intrinsically dialogical and relational—not something we do on our own.

IMITATE: Imitation here does not mean to mimic, so much as to act. To "imitate" means to express and share the love that is already growing within us. Imitation means to be transformed and to participate in a gaze of love that becomes active in us. Imitation includes all of the ways that the contemplative, relational grounding we are cultivating gives us the capacity for purposeful action in the world around us.

FOR REFLECTION:

1. Gazing requires a space within the heart to receive what we see and to "embrace" what we see. Poverty helps create this space because when we are free of things we possess or that possess us we are able to see more clearly and to receive what we see within us.

Thinking about your own habits and your life circumstances, what would you say "possesses" you?

2. The gaze is a "movement toward"—a movement toward God, toward the authentic self, toward the image of God embedded within us, and toward the God who has loved us all into being. What holds you back from that movement of the Spirit calling you toward God?

3. How would your relationship with God and your very life flourish with a deeper, more continual practice of gazing, considering, and contemplating?

The Revolution of Tenderness

When Francis died in 1226, his movement was already somewhat divided. A significant number of newer brothers had little interest in living at the margins and lacked the radical connections with the poor that had informed Francis's sense of who God was. Instead, they were dedicated to preaching and wanted university education to prepare themselves. As they saw it, mendicancy was not an act of solidarity so much as it was an impediment to their pastoral formation. An excellent case could be made that, without Clare and her stalwart commitment to radical poverty, the original vision of Francis might have been lost over time. In point of historical fact, the male branch of the order struggled with the question of poverty in ways that the female branch did not. The steady, even course of the Poor Ladies through the thirteenth century was due, in large part, to Clare's visionary leadership, her fidelity, and her firm commitment to daily silence in the presence of God. In this sense, Clare provides a poignant example of how sometimes radical fidelity to basic ideals and values is what becomes revolutionary over time.

Scholarship of the last 20-30 years allows us to see Clare as an active and critical contributor to the Franciscan legacy, equal in charismatic authority to Francis. Clare's vision of poverty was one of active solidarity with the poor. Poverty was not borne for the sake of poverty, but as an act of affiliation with those who had nothing and lived in amidst the dangers and precarity of life outside the city walls, allowing the providence and generosity of God to shine forth. In Clare's community, any money that a Poor Lady had upon entry was not given to the community; it was given to the poor. There was never any question of the community having a surplus, much less an endowment to guarantee their stability. The whole point was to live in the same precarity that defined the life of the majority of medieval people, especially those with nowhere to go. Francis himself admired Clare's steadfastness and felt the need, from time to time, to encourage her not to fast with such intensity, even as, toward the end of his life during his stay at San Damiano in 1225, he explicitly encouraged Clare to embrace poverty as a spiritual gift.

For Clare, poverty was essential, because it created space for God. The absence of material things centered daily life around God and allowed the beauty of creation to support a disposition of gratitude and generosity. Communal simplicity supported each woman's orientation to God and amplified her relational intimacy. Writing to Agnes of Prague, her sister in Christ across the Alps, Clare calls Agnes, her "most beloved sister, or should I say, Lady worthy of great respect, because you are the spouse and the mother and the sister of my Lord Jesus Christ and are beautifully adorned with the banners of an undefiled virginity and a most holy poverty..." (Clare's First Letter to Agnes of Prague). For Clare, poverty always enhances our lives, since it is the primary way that we express our desire to live in greater intimacy, with God and others. In this sense, poverty erases boundaries and always enriches us.

Clare spent over 40 years of her life in the space of San Damiano—the same space where Francis had first received a sense of his vocation to "rebuild My home" and create a community of care that replicated the earliest community around Jesus. Clare not only safeguarded Francis's legacy; she embodied a generosity of spirit that she learned directly from God, developing it into a God-centered way of life. Clare's fidelity to the gospel vision of poverty and simplicity was both an anchor of stability and a compass for genuine intimacy with God. Every step away from pride and vanity was a step toward wisdom, the gifts of the Spirit, and the embrace of a Companion whose presence brings joy and fruition. As we seek to understand the element of metanoia that we are calling the revolution of tenderness, Clare gives us a strong model for how to create, develop, and turn over to a new generation a true spiritual legacy.

FOR REFLECTION:

1. What spiritual practices do you engage that create greater intimacy with God?

2. Have you ever known simplicity to enhance the quality of an encounter or experience?

3. In what ways are you a spiritual teacher to people around you?

Moments of Metanoia
in Dorothy Day

"The biggest challenge of the day is:
how to bring about a revolution of the heart,
a revolution that has to start with each one of us."

The Unexpected Invitation

Dorothy Day was born at the turn of the twentieth-century, in 1897. The daughter of a journalist, her family moved several times, and, as a young child, she was exposed to many social issues in the world. She lived in Oakland during the time of the 1906 earthquake in San Francisco, for example, and she went with her mother into the city to provide shelter, first aid, and other care to its victims. The sight of temporary shelters, soup kitchens, and the spontaneous sharing of basic necessities made a deep impression on her, as she wondered why this kind of collaboration and mutual care happened only in times of crisis and not as an ordinary way of life.

During her adolescence and early college years, Dorothy Day's awareness of the plight of immigrants and the working poor grew; this led her to a deep commitment to the cause of social justice in all forms. An intelligent, socially engaged woman, she worked actively with others to gain American women's right to vote, and she was imprisoned several times in this struggle. She left college after two years, wanting to put her natural curiosity and her skills as a writer to work as a newspaper reporter. She focused on the lives and struggles of America's working poor, and she advocated for change.

Dorothy Day's family home was not religious, and in college her friends were political and social activists who did not have a framework of faith for their perspectives on social justice. Nonetheless, in her childhood, Dorothy was exposed to the deep faith of many of her friends' mothers. In her autobiography, The Long Loneliness, and other writings, Dorothy describes poignant moments in which seeing these women in prayer sparked a genuine affection for them and made enough of an impression that, as she struggled for an overarching worldview and relational framework for her desire for a more just society, she sensed a deep need for something that stirred the human heart and could guide the individual and social conscience. It was not so much that Dorothy Day sought religion; it was more that she had a longing for meaning in her life, and she knew that relationship with God was possible because she had deep-seated memories of people whose lives were sustained through prayer.

Dorothy's socialist and anarchist friends were puzzled by her spiritual instincts. But with deepening reflection and radical honesty, Dorothy came to understand that the kind of human community she sought required a grounding in love and a commitment to community that she found impossible to sustain without a rich relationship with God. This instinct to love only deepened when, unexpectedly, she found herself expecting a child—an unexpected invitation in so many ways. Dorothy was happily in love with Forster Batterham, a botanist she had met through friends in New York. They lived together for four years and only began a process of ultimate separation upon the birth of their child, Tamar Teresa. From the day that she knew she was pregnant, Dorothy understood the gift of becoming a mother as a direct act of God. She had survived a backstreet abortion and had been told she could never have a baby.

Forster, too, was ready to become a father. But he resisted marriage, especially because Dorothy insisted upon being married in the Catholic Church and baptizing their child. It was the moral grounding of relationship with God that Dorothy wanted, and she was unable to locate that relationship anywhere but the Catholic Church, despite the fact that her needs alienated Forster and gave her little initial joy. In *From Union Square to Rome*, Dorothy describes this time:

> My child was born in March at the end of a harsh winter. In December I had to come in from the country and take a little apartment in town. It was good to be there, close to friends, close to a church where I could stop and pray. I read the Imitation of Christ a great deal. I knew that I was going to have my child baptized a Catholic, cost what it may. I knew that I was not going to have her floundering through many years as I had done, doubting and hesitating, undisciplined and amoral. I felt it was the greatest thing I could do for a child. For myself, I prayed for the gift of faith. I was sure, yet not sure. I postponed the day of decision...
>
> I had become convinced that I would become a Catholic, and yet I felt I was betraying the class to which I belonged, you my brothers and sisters, the workers, the poor of the world, the class which Christ most loved and spent his life with.

And later, in *The Long Loneliness*, Dorothy describes her decisions, as a young mother, to the choice "quite literally, between God and man."

> It was years before I woke up without that longing for a face pressed against my breast, an arm about my shoulder. The

sense of loss was there. I never was so unhappy, never felt so great the sense of loneliness. No matter how many times I gave up mother, father, husband, brother, daughter, for His sake, I had to do it over again.

For Dorothy, the initial stage of metanoia—what we have been calling an unexpected invitation—brought as much darkness as it did light, because her path forward had to be created, one step at a time, and because, until she found companions and built community, she could not move forward. Her early life is a reminder of those graces which are seen and appreciated far more in hindsight than in the moment that they are given.

FOR REFLECTION:

1. Has your life ever come down to a simple, but radical choice? If so, what was that like, and how did your eventual decision bear fruit?

2. In what ways do you currently choose toward God? Have you asked God for guidance about other ways to choose toward God?

Eyes to See

For several years after her own baptism and that of her daughter Tamar Teresa, Dorothy Day felt little joy. She struggled to find a path of meaningful self-expression, solidarity, and service and spent several years in Mexico before returning to the United States. In December 1932 Dorothy Day covered a hunger march in Washington, DC for Commonweal and America magazines. While in Washington, she visited the basilica of the Immaculate Conception and prayed for guidance for her future.

Upon her return to New York City, where her sister and brother-in-law lived, she met a man who would become her lifelong friend and collaborator, Peter Maurin. Over months of supper conversations, Maurin, a Frenchman with a background in Catholic social teaching, shared with Dorothy his vision of how to embody gospel principles. She was in strong agreement, not only with the principles Maurin articulated but with the urgency he felt to get started. They began what became the Catholic Worker movement with an effort where Dorothy's skills and experiences could easily bear fruit: a newspaper, sold on the streets for a penny a copy (and given away when people could not afford the penny). *The Catholic Worker* newspaper sought to bring to light the struggles of ordinary workers, the injustices they suffered, and the many ways that the gospel provided concrete suggestions for how to reshape the world. (Articles from *The Catholic Worker*, many of which were written by Dorothy Day and Peter Maurin, are available at www.thecatholicnewsarchive.org.)

In many ways, Dorothy did not need "eyes to see" the challenges of her day. What she needed were the hands and hearts of people who cared enough to share their material provisions, their talents, and their energies. New York City, like so many urban centers, was full of people unable to find work or feed their families: the breadlines were long, the winters were cold, and the only way through the misery of the 1930s was to build community. Dorothy Day was a single mother who had always been enough of a social and political activist to have strong moral sensitivities. Her friendship with Peter Maurin and a growing circle of others emboldened her to develop a larger vision of action that integrated social principles with the gospel and turned words into deeds.

FOR REFLECTION:

1. If you were to begin a new work with God—one that capitalized on your strengths and the wisdom you have achieved at this point in your life—what would it look like?

2. How can your deepest principles be put into more concrete actions that effect positive change in the community or world around you?

Radical Departure/Beyond Borders

*It was not enough to convey by word of mouth
in round table discussion the program of a new social order.
It was necessary to embrace voluntary poverty and the
Works of Mercy, to feed, clothe and shelter people
who were in need.*

- Dorothy Day, *The Catholic Worker,* May 1939

The next step of the Catholic Worker movement, opening houses of hospitality for the homeless and disenfranchised, was not long in coming. She began by renting an amalgam of apartments, one in a condemned tenement on Fourth Street and another on Fifteenth, until finally a Catholic Worker "headquarters" on Mott Street came together, with twenty rooms, a few flats, two storefront areas for food distribution, a reading room, and a space for community gatherings. From the beginning the Catholic Worker house was a social experiment. In fact, Dorothy characteristically avoided regimentation and dictating rules over a population that she felt had already suffered and endured so much. Her point (which she often had to defend over other approaches) was that Jesus modeled radical acceptance, and therefore the Catholic Worker houses would model radical hospitality. Room was always made for people, even if there was no actual bed space, since "anything was better than being on the streets in the cold and snow."

In every instance of receiving a guest, Dorothy Day would say that the community was "making room for Christ," an act that she insisted that each and every person of faith was obliged to do. In her reflection "Room for Christ," written in Advent, she once wrote:

> It is no use to say that we are born two thousand years too late to give room to Christ. Nor will those who live at the end of the world have been born too late. Christ is always with us, always asking for room in our hearts. But now it is with the voice of our contemporaries that he speaks, with the eyes of store clerks, factory workers and children that he gazes; with the hands of office workers, slum dwellers and suburban housewives that he gives. It is with the feet of soldiers and tramps that he walks, and with the heart of anyone in need that he longs for shelter. And giving shelter or food to anyone who asks for it, or needs it, is giving it to Christ. (Dorothy Day, "Room for Christ," *The Catholic Worker,* December 1, 1945. Available at https://catholicworker.org/416-2/)

Dorothy's insistence upon making room for everyone required accommodation, both from volunteers and from outsiders who did not appreciate the chaos of transience and the apparent lack of discipline in the community. Neighbors "bear with our breadline which every morning for two and a half years now has lined up along the street for a block and a half, impeding traffic, blocking doorways on rainy days when the men huddle in the shadow of the buildings to escape the wet," she wrote in an article describing life in the first houses of hospitality. (See *The Catholic Worker*, May 1939. 1, 3, 4.)

Dorothy's commitment to hospitality was broad and deep. She constantly tried to make room for all seeking shelter or aid and she put no time limit to a person's stay at a Catholic Worker house. Some people would stay a day or a week and eventually find work or a different situation. Others, especially those who were disabled or who suffered mental illness, might stay indefinitely. Here is Dorothy Day's explicit description:

> We believe that when we undertake the responsibility of caring for someone who comes to us, we are accepting it for good… Some have been with us for five years and probably will die with us. Some are with us for only a few months and then find jobs and leave to make room for others. Many are unemployable and we must take care of them as we would a member of the family who cannot find work. Usually there are tasks about the house which occupy them for a few hours a day so that their lives can be given some aim and continuity. (*The Catholic Worker*, May 1939. 1, 3, 4.)

In the end, the constancy of the Catholic Worker community's witness won people over: the community could always be counted on to take in one more person, to extend the meal several more plates, to make room, to find clothing, to do whatever it took to meet a need. In this way Dorothy Day and Peter Maurin's vision moved beyond borders and invited others to know the work of uplifting accompaniment that Jesus modeled. They sought by word and example to explore what Christian discipleship looks like in the face of social inequality, and gradually hundreds were drawn into the movement. Dorothy Day's writing as well as her lifestyle was radical, simple, direct, sincere, and deeply committed, even as it was never easy. As she describes with a simple eloquence, so characteristic of her writing:

But daily, hourly, to give up our own possessions and especially to subordinate our own impulses and wishes to others—these are hard, hard things; and I don't think they ever get any easier. You can strip yourself, you can be stripped, but still you will reach out like an octopus to seek your own comfort, your untroubled time, your ease, your refreshment. It may mean books or music—the gratification of the inner sense—or it may mean food and drink, coffee and cigarettes. The one kind of giving up is no easier than the other. (*Loaves and Fishes*, p. 84)

Dorothy's rigorous example of solidarity, peacemaking, and social advocacy inspired thousands and the Catholic Worker movement of voluntary poverty and solidarity lives on today.

FOR REFLECTION:

1. Dorothy Day's description of self-stripping above is both poignant and a reminder of the radical self stripping of Francis of Assisi centuries before. How have you engaged the process of self-stripping? What is left for you to purge from your life, so that you are more centered on God and the human community?

2. How have you engaged what Dorothy Day calls above "making room for Christ"? What have you learned from such experiences?

Radiating Love

We have all known the long loneliness
and we have learned that the only solution
is love and that love comes with community.

- The Long Loneliness

Like Oscar Romero, Dorothy Day is another person who makes explicit and visible the integral links between love and justice. For Dorothy Day, to call oneself Christian is to aspire to both a courageous goodness and a love that opens possibility for others. Every principle embodied in the Catholic Worker movement was rooted in love, acceptance, service, humility, and prayer:

Love and ever more love is the only solution to every problem that comes up. If we love each other enough, we will bear with each other's faults and burdens. If we love enough, we are going to light that fire in the hearts of others. And it is love that will burn out the sins and hatreds that sadden us. It is love that will make us want to do great things for each other. No sacrifice and no suffering will then seem too much. (Dorothy Day, *House of Hospitality*, chapter 14 [1939], available at: https://catholicworker.org/449-html/)

As young people gravitated toward Catholic Worker communities, they would often find Dorothy at work peeling potatoes, cleaning bathrooms, hoeing and weeding in the gardens, or providing a listening ear. Dorothy expressed love in quotidian tasks and was sometimes mistaken for a resident because her clothing always came from the leftovers of the community. Like Francis of Assisi, for Dorothy, love always came down to simple acts of humanity that dignified the community and proved to people that they were not alone.

FOR REFLECTION:

1. What has love empowered you to do for others?

2. What concrete practices help you keep the fire of love alive?

The Revolution of Tenderness

As both a writer and a reformer, Dorothy Day consciously built communities that extended the work of the gospel through time and space. She approached this work very simply and often referred to the "corporal works of mercy" as a core gospel activity in which all could (and should) participate.

Dorothy Day was a compelling writer and author of hundreds of newspaper articles in *The Catholic Worker*. She wrote many fine and under-appreciated autobiographical pieces, most notably *The Long Loneliness* (1952). This was neither her first nor her last attempt to tell the story of her life, especially from the vantage point of her relationship with God. Repeatedly she described the challenge to live with integrity, simplicity and solidarity with the poor and the ways that she found God along the way: *From Union Square to Rome* (1938), *On Pilgrimage* (1948) and *Loaves and Fishes* (1963). Because Dorothy Day was so deeply engaged socially, much of her writing includes reference to very specific historical events and eras. But her writings always circle back to timeless moral principles, making them continually applicable in the 21st century.

The hallmarks of the Catholic Worker Movement were solidarity, peace-making, hospitality and enactment of the works of mercy, both in daily accompaniment of those in need and in advocacy for social change. *The Catholic Worker* newspaper, published monthly, served as a vehicle to inform, generate dialogue, and extend consideration of moral issues throughout society.

Dorothy Day believed strongly in embodying the principles she espoused not only in how she lived but also in where she stood. She rarely missed a protest, especially as an advocate for peace, and she strongly supported the right of young people not to participate in war. Part of Dorothy Day's impact included the ways that she modeled the need for a consistent ethic of dignity in church and society. Dorothy Day's integrity and tenacity was, in many ways, the backbone of both the Catholic Worker movement and *The Catholic Worker* newspaper. Her clarity, authority, and charism had a deep and broad reach.

A significant number of Catholics growing up in the 1950s, 1960s and 1970s were strongly impacted by the Catholic Worker Movement, especially since it gave young people a way to put Catholic social teaching into practice in concrete ways. They lived and ministered in Houses of Hospitalities; they labored on the movement's farms or in summer camps; they got the newspaper out monthly and supported the movement's mission to focus on the plight of the poor, the worker, the migrant without ever reducing the dignity of each person or the uniqueness of each story.

Even today 200 Catholic Worker communities around the world remain committed to nonviolence, voluntary poverty, prayer, and hospitality for the homeless, exiled, hungry, and forsaken. In Dorothy Day, we see a call to human goodness, rooted in gospel principles and human solidarity, guided by the love of God, that leads us be the community God created us to be.

We are all called to be saints, St. Paul says, and we might as well get over our bourgeois fear of the name. We might also get used to recognizing the fact that there is some of the saint in all of us. Inasmuch as we are growing, putting off the old person and putting on Christ, there is some of the saint, the holy, the divine right there…. We are all called to be saints. Sometimes we don't see them around us, sometimes their sanctity is obscured by the human, but they are there nonetheless." (Dorothy Day, *The Third Hour*, 1949)

FOR REFLECTION:

1. How does Dorothy Day's observation ("Inasmuch as we are growing, putting off the old person and putting on Christ, there is some of the saint, the holy, the divine right there… We are all called to be saints.") resonate with you?

2. Having considered the lives of our first three faces of metanoia, what does holiness now mean to you? How do you see yourself growing in holiness? What supports, individually and communally, do you need in order to continue to grow in holiness?

Moments of Metanoia
in Oscar Romero

If at some point they take away from us the radio, suspend the newspaper, forbid us to speak, kill all of us priests and the bishop also, and you remain, a people without priests, each one of you must be a microphone of God, each one of you must be a messenger, a prophet.

- Oscar Romero, Homily of July 8, 1979

The Unexpected Invitation

Oscar Romero was born on August 15, 1917 into a family of modest means. He received a simple education and was trained in carpentry, until he declared his hope to become a priest. He entered seminary and eventually went to Rome to study at the Gregorian. His higher education was interrupted by World War II, and he returned to El Salvador, working as a parish priest in San Miguel for over 20 years before slowly moving up the ranks of the church in El Salvador, becoming a bishop in 1970.

El Salvador is the smallest and most densely populated country in Central America. At the time that Romero became bishop, 30% of its population was landless. Workers were exploited by plantation owners, often making just a dollar or two per day for their labor in coffee and cotton fields. Over the course of the

1970s the crisis over land ownership, just wages for agricultural workers, and equal access to education and social services escalated. By the time that Romero was appointed archbishop of El Salvador in February 1977, it was difficult to ignore rising tensions across the country.

Because he was seen as introverted and bookish, people expected Romero to be an unremarkable church leader. But in his three years as archbishop, Romero experienced, taught, and modeled a genuine conversion to the reign of God – a conversion brought about by his accompaniment of the crucified Christ in the poor of El Salvador. To walk with Romero is to be introduced to the ways that God continually works in and with us, calling us to grow and to change. Romero teaches us the power of the incarnation and how we are called to participate in God's ongoing incarnation in our world today.

Romero's unexpected invitation to metanoia was deeply painful: shortly after Romero became archbishop, Fr. Rutilio Grande, a close Jesuit friend who had been in seminary with Romero, was assassinated. Grande had walked closely with the poor in his parish in Aguilares. For Grande, economic exploitation was not a theoretical problem: it was the daily agony of parents in his own parish losing children to diarrhea and dehydration because there was no clean water, people working in fields and not earning enough to feed their families. He spoke to Romero about the need for the church to express its concern for the poor by addressing their needs and accompanying them more directly in their poverty. Grande wanted the church to use its moral influence and authority in prophetic preaching capable of moving people to reject the injustices built into El Salvador's social, political, and economic structures.

Romero knew Grande to be a person of integrity with an intense and loving concern for the people under his care. When Romero saw his friend's body laid out for burial next to the aging campesino and young boy killed with him, the reality and urgency of innocent suffering pierced him to the bone. Rutilio Grande's death instilled in Romero a very specific sense of his pastoral responsibility: he was to listen, to understand the lived experience of his people, to help them to see God in their midst, and to exhort all Salvadorans to fidelity to the gospel's call to dignity, equality, and love. As he stood with poor villagers around the three corpses, Romero realized that the church existed to serve the poor and be a voice for the voiceless.

FOR REFLECTION:

1.   Have you experienced a loss that taught you something about life? Reflect on some of what it taught you, and consider whether or not you have responded to those life lessons since the loss.

2.   There are moments in history when the loss of one visionary leader leads to the emergence of another or in another way of sharing leadership within a community. Reflect on one of those moments, whether it is in history or in the history of a church, organization or community that you have been a part of. How have you experienced the movement of the Spirit in such shifts?

Eyes to See

The next two steps of metanoia proceeded rapidly and decisively from Romero's sense of vocation as a bishop. We will explore this moment of metanoia, "Eyes to See," from two vantage points: first, what Romero had already been given eyes to see through the murder of his friend and colleague, Rutilio

Grande, and second, from what he continued to learn in the first year of his life as archbishop, as he made more and more changes in the church's way of accompanying the poor and denouncing injustice.

First we examine Romero's immediate response in light of the death of Rutilio Grande and the two members of his parish who had been in the car with him on that fatal day of Grande's assassination. In a move both symbolic and significant, Romero refused to participate in any governmental function until the murders had been investigated and justice had been served. This decision was a dramatic break from tradition and precedent, but for Romero it was essential that the church not be seen to endorse, much less bless, the actions of an unjust and repressive government. He gathered people from various sectors of the church—priests, vowed religious, and lay leaders—and consulted with them about how to proceed in the days following the assassination. As a result, he decided to suspend classes in all Catholic schools for three days, calling for prayer, study, and reflection, using documents from the Second Vatican Council and the Latin American Bishops' conference in Medellín in 1968. Romero also decided that on the Sunday following the assassination there would be a single mass in all of El Salvador, held at the cathedral in the capital, and it would be a funeral mass for Rutilio Grande and the two others. In this way, Romero sought both to honor the life of the fallen and oblige the entirety of the Salvadoran church to acknowledge the moral disaster of pastoral leaders being targeted for violence in the course of their work for God. To the secretary of the papal nuncio in El Salvador, Romero explained that the extraordinary actions of violence in the country required the church to make an equally extraordinary response of denunciation and evangelization.

This early principle became Romero's way of proceeding as a pastoral leader: he countered violence with prophetic words that denounced injustice, preached an alternative, and provided hope that God was not only watching over the situation in El Salvador but also was present in the suffering and anguish of its people. In all things, Romero sought to evangelize—that is, to allow the Gospel to shed light on human circumstances. Romero began to scrutinize every church ritual and decision, wanting to ensure that, in every way, the Church made an authentic option for the poor and used its authority to become a voice for the voiceless. And a backlash of criticism erupted. This, too, gave Romero "eyes to see" what the Gospel and the crucified Christ were up against in Salvadoran society. Knowing that his duty, as a leader of the church, was to give others eyes to see the truth of the gospel, especially as that gospel was coming alive in the world around them, Romero dedicated himself to this very specific way of evangelizing.

In his second pastoral letter as archbishop of El Salvador, written on August 2, 1977 for the feast day of the Transfiguration, Romero reflected on the work of evangelization as he experienced it in the first five months of his time as archbishop. He took the occasion to hold up for all to see what he was observing as he worked to align church practice with the values of the reign of God.

> Some have rejoiced, because they sense the Church close to their problems and pains, and it gives them hope that the Church participates in their joys.

> Others have been offended or saddened, because they sense, in the new attitude of the church, a clear demand that they, too, must change and be converted. And every conversion is difficult and painful, because the change that is demanded does not refer only to the way we think but also to the way we live.

> Many Catholics of good will have been disappointed or perhaps have even had doubts about following in the actual

footsteps of the Church and instead have preferred to take refuge in the security of a tradition that refuses to evolve.

Others, more moved by selfish interests than by purity of heart and fidelity to the Church, have... attacked all that is closest to the heart of Christ's Church by saying that we are being unfaithful to the Gospel.

But thanks be to God that there are innumerable sons and daughters of the church: priests, vowed religious, and laypeople sincerely committed to the demands of the Reign that Jesus preached, who have been strengthened in their faith, hope and Christian commitment and, along with the Church, just like the apostle, they say: "let us go, too, and die with him." (John 11:16).

(The entirety of Romero's letter, along with his other letters and his homilies, are available in both English and Spanish at the website of the Romero Trust. They are well worth reading, and I am citing small portions of them here. Specifically, the above paragraphs of the Transfiguration pastoral letter provide a powerful way to locate our own response to the challenge of the Gospel to be converted and to accompany those who suffer unjustly.)

In his book, *Archbishop Romero: Memories and Reflections*, Jon Sobrino describes the core elements of Romero's early conversion and all that he learned, as he gained eyes to see how to be a pastoral leader amidst violence and oppression:

In a brief time, Archbishop Romero had to learn to make important decisions... He had to learn to maintain a dialogue with his priests. He had to learn serenity, lest he do things that would make the situation worse. He had to learn boldness, in order to be able to confront and denounce the powerful. He had to learn to give the people hope, and receive from them their suffering, their faith, and their commitment. Within himself, he had to learn his faith in the God of the poor, who was also the God greater than all else, greater than the church itself, which was gradually becoming his cross. He had to learn that there is nothing more important than the Reign of God—that there was nothing more important than life, hope, love, and a communion of sisters and brothers. He had to learn that the church's place is among the suffering poor, immersed in the reality of the crucified peoples. (Sobrino, *Archbishop Romero: Memories and Reflections*, p. 23)

Sobrino saw, in Romero, a genuine conversion that gave Romero inner strength and a joyful energy for his work. As Sobrino helpfully reconstructs these early months of Romero's time as archbishop, he shows us that it involved a great deal of learning. This learning was rooted in deep listening. The church's mission to accompany the poor had to be informed by the reality of the poor. As he spent more time listening, Romero gained a deeper understanding of the social reality that moved him to make decisions that shaped the Salvadoran church and supported those who were being trampled down.

FOR REFLECTION:

1. How do you maintain access with the lives of those who can helpfully inform you about the injustices in your own community and society?

2. Reviewing the list of "lessons" that Sobrino describes in Romero's first months as archbishop, how have you engaged similar learning—of serenity, of boldness, of prioritizing the reign of God above all else? Which

of the lessons do you still have to learn, and how will you engage that learning process?

Radical Departure/Beyond Barriers

During his three years as bishop, Romero's decisions in favor of radical solidarity with the poor moved him beyond the norms that bishops before him had observed. His departure from the expectations of wealthy Salvadorans in the church began early. In February 1977, Romero chose not to live in a palatial residence built in his honor and instead took up residence at the Hospital of Divina Providencia. This hospital, run by a community of religious sisters, offered him simplicity, silence, and prayerful support for his daily work. After his death, sisters there described how the light in his room would often be on very late at night, as he prayed, wrote homilies, and corresponded with people in El Salvador and beyond.

With any number of concrete actions, Romero was able to reach beyond barriers and express, in word and deed, a practice of presence that affirmed and supported people's participation in the incarnate presence of Christ in the Christian community. Nowhere was this more evident than in Romero's outreach to the people of the town of Aguilares, where Rutilio Grande had ministered.

On May 19, 1977, the army, following the declaration of a state of emergency, went into Aguilares and expelled the three remaining Jesuits, desecrated the church, and set up a roadblock that denied entry and exit to all. Both Romero and the papal nuncio were refused access to Aguilares and its church. A month later, on June 19, the army drove everyone out of Aguilares altogether. At that point Romero was determined to bring his personal presence to the terrorized people, both to denounce the violence and to inspire their courage, fidelity, and inner strength.

Romero began his mass in Aguilares on that day: "I have the job of picking up the trampled, the corpses, and all that persecution of the church dumps along the road... a people disgracefully humiliated and sacrificed.... We are truly with you, and your pain is the church's pain." This depth of solidarity and personal presence, expressed with absolute sincerity and transparent love, was something that people came to anticipate from Romero, and it gave them an entirely new sense of what a Christian community could and should become.

In his personal diary, Romero expressed a core principle which quickly became the central focus of his ministry: modeling what poverty and simplicity of spirit before God looks like and exhorting all to "nakedly follow the naked Christ." (This phrase, originally written by Jerome in the 4th century, was known and deliberately repeated throughout the Middle Ages by many authors, especially those in the Franciscan tradition. It represents a posture of humble self-stripping before God—a material, emotional and spiritual poverty that allows us to approach God simply, sincerely, and totally.). As Romero later wrote in his journal on January 10, 1979:

> The poor person is the one who has been converted to God and puts all his faith in God, and the rich person is one who has not been converted to God and puts his confidence in idols: money, power, material things... Our work should be directed toward converting ourselves and all people to this authentic meaning of poverty. (*A Shepherd's Diary*, p. 125.)

Consistent with this mission, Romero suspended repairs on the cathedral of San Salvador in 1978. He felt it was scandalous to use Church money for something ostentatious when so many poorer Salvadorans lacked food and potable drinking water for their families.

But by the time of that decision, Romero had already been articulating the mission of the church as one of prophetic solidarity. In his Holy Thursday homily from 1977, several weeks after the death of Rutilio Grande, he preached:

> You are the prophets of the world... You have to announce like the prophets, like a prophetic people anointed by the same Spirit that anointed Christ, the wonders of God in the world, to encourage the good that is already in our world and to denounce and condemn evil. (Oscar Romero, Homily of April 7, 1977)

Statements like this, preached so early in the three years of his archbishopric, should signal for us the fundamental orientation to a justice that radiates from the heart of God into the entirety of creation, felling barriers and obstacles and drawing people together in their common purpose to build up the reign of God.

> The church is concerned about the rights of people... and about any life that is in danger... The church is concerned about those who cannot speak, those who suffer, those who are tortured or silenced. To be concerned is not political activity. Quite simply, politics is now "touching the altar," it is now touching the moral life of the people, and so the church has the right to speak. It cannot remain silent. (Oscar Romero, Homily of May 8, 1977)

> Preaching that does not denounce sin is not the preaching of the Gospel. Preaching that makes sinners feel good and entrenches them in their sinful state is a betrayal of the Gospel's call... Preaching that awakens and enlightens people, like a light that is turned on when someone is sleeping naturally disturbs us, but it wakes us up! That is the preaching of Christ, who says, "Wake up! Be converted!" This is also the church's authentic preaching. Naturally, sisters and brothers, such preaching will encounter conflict;

it loses worldly prestige; it bothers people and will surely be persecuted. The church's preaching cannot get along with the powers of darkness and sin. "Be converted" is the call that Christ extends to us. (Oscar Romero, Homily of January 22, 1978)

FOR REFLECTION:

1. Romero's embodiment of the "mission" of the church models both a departure from church tradition and "protocol" in favor of the formation of a community where everyone belongs and everyone matters. Consider some of the ways that human dignity is denied today, listing both some examples of the denial of human dignity and alternative ways that human dignity can be restored and defended.

2. Another way to describe the deep solidarity that Romero preached and modeled as archbishop could be derived from words spoken by Greg Boyle. In his work with former gang members in Los Angeles, Boyle speaks of creating and collaborating together in "a world where there is no 'us' and 'them.' Just 'us.'" Take a moment to imagine a world where there is "no 'us' and 'them.' Just 'us.'" What boundaries would dissolve? What problems that currently seem insurmountable might have solutions? How does confidence in the human capacity to collaborate change our feelings and perception about life?

Radiating Love

As we have already seen, Romero was tireless in living out a vocation of prophetic action on behalf of the poor. His Sunday homilies were broadcast over the radio to people all across the nation and served as light, hope, and inspiration to thousands. Romero's homilies were a constant reminder of the prophetic nature of the church but also an ongoing invitation to all to participate in the work of the church: to build up the reign of God, to lift up those trampled down by injustice, to sow seeds of wisdom and goodness that would bear fruit in a more just world.

> These homilies want to be the voice of this people. They want to be the voice of those who have no voice. And therefore, without a doubt, they bother those who have too much of a voice. This poor voice will find an echo in those who, as I have said before, love truth and truly love our beloved people. (Oscar Romero, Homily of July 29, 1979)

One of the special gifts that Romero shared with his contemporaries and those who came after him is his way of integrating love and justice. Romero makes clear that love is neither a feeling nor an emotion. It is a way of living, acting, choosing, moving toward, and being with. Love is shown by deeds far more than words, and it can never be separated from the impulse to justice, decency, kindness, and equity. As Paul suggests in 1 Corinthians 13, love also engenders hope. It creates ways forward through its invitation to dignity and its desire to enhance the life of others. We cannot say we love someone whose dignity we deny by our actions. Oscar Romero embodied the integral connections between love and justice.

A poignant example of the love that does justice was Romero's decision to create a space of safety for those impacted by political disappearance. Because more and more people were being disappeared—that is, taken from their homes, schools, workplaces, or off the streets and forced into clandestine prisons, where they were often tortured and sometimes left for dead—there needed to be a trustworthy central office where people could report the disappearance of their relatives, gather evidence for legal proceedings, leave a photograph in case an unidentified corpse appeared, and receive moral support in their grief, loss, and outrage. Tutela Legal provided these services, as well as actively investigating cases of disappearance and abuse.

Located in the chancery offices of the archdiocese, Tutela Legal was both a safe haven for people wanting to report their loved ones missing and an autonomous organization able to act independently of pressures from the government and military. In addition to recording information about human rights violations, Tutela Legal promoted and defended international human rights law, and reported atrocities to local and international media outlets, so that organizations like Amnesty International and others could provide support.

The work of Tutela Legal was a critical facet of pastoral accompaniment as political violence increased, and it was a concrete manifestation of what Romero preached about maintaining an authentic Christian witness that opposed political repression:

> It must be made very clear that if what one wants to do is collaborate with a pseudo-peace, a false order based on repression and fear, we must remember that the only order and the only peace that God wants is the one based on truth and justice. And faced with this divide, our option... is clear, have no doubt. We will obey the order of God before the order of men. (Oscar Romero, Homily of July 1, 1979)

In return for his work of evangelization in word and deed, Oscar Romero received death threats, and the radio station which broadcast his homilies was bombed. In his homilies, he reflected:

The only thing that consoles me is that Christ… was also misunderstood and they called him a rebel and they sentenced him to death, as they are threatening me these days.

In March of 1980 he made a public appeal to the U.S. to stop sending military aid to the government of El Salvador. A day later, on March 24, 1980, his life was interrupted by an assassin's bullet while he celebrated Mass in the chapel at the Hospital of the Divine Providencia. His life had come full circle.

FOR REFLECTION:

1. How have you experienced the need for courage in today's world? Does your Christian orientation provide you with the inner strength you need for prophetic action? How and with whom can you strengthen that prophetic witness?

2. Call to mind people in history who have taken great risks in order to advance the cause of human goodness. Make a list of them, and consider the impact that their lives had, whether in concrete social change or in terms of the communities they left behind.

The Revolution of Tenderness

There is a Spanish word, *entregar*, which means to give oneself over to something. It is not so much a "surrendering" of the self, as it is a handing over, a freely chosen self-dedication to others.

During the difficult years of Salvadoran history in the 1970s and 1980s, those who worked on behalf of, suffered with, and tried to change the plight of the poor were said to have "turned themselves over" to them, in a full and totally committed way. *Entregado*—a person who has turned over the self to God and to others—fully describes Oscar Romero, from the moment that he took in the reality and brutality of his friend Rutilio Grande's assassination.

With each passing day after that, Romero's commitment to God in the poor deepened. In many ways, Romero's life models how metanoia, the fullness of self-dedication to God and to the reign of God, is to *entregarse*—to turn oneself over to God especially in the incarnate God present at the margins of society. Throughout the first four stages of metanoia we have seen this process at work, but it is here, in the stage of "revolution"—the turning over of a way of life and the space in which the legacy of our lives plays out into the next generation—where Romero's *entrega* becomes most poignant.

Romero sensed that he would join those disappeared or assassinated. He did not seek martyrdom, but with each loss of a colleague to political disappearance, he understood experientially the potential consequences of following the gospel's call to prophetic action. He often took up the topic of persecution and martyrdom in his homilies, and he emphasized that the love of God expressed in Christian witness to truth and justice could ultimately never be killed.

> Martyrdom is a grace that I don't believe I deserve… But if God accepts the sacrifice of my life, then may my blood be a seed of liberty and sign of the hope that will soon be a reality.

If Romero never saw his prophetic witness as anything singular or exceptional, he also saw that his violent death would not be either. He saw himself (just as he saw others) as participating in the body of Christ—a body that bears witness, uplifts, embodies goodness, suffers, and is resurrected. For example, in his homily of July 8, 1979 he said:

> I have never felt I was a prophet in the sense of being the only prophet of the people. I know that you and I, the people of God, together, compose the prophetic people. I am happy to say that, thank God, there is a prophetic awakening in our archdiocese: in the base church community, in prayer and study groups, and in this critical awareness that is developing in our Christianity, which will be a Christianity of the herd no longer; now it means to be a Christianity of awareness.

Even beyond death, Oscar Romero invites us today to see Christianity as a source of ethical reflection, personal and social conversion, and commitment to the transformation of self and society, so that, whatever the cost, the values of the reign of God that Jesus preached and modeled are never lost.

FOR REFLECTION:

Romero's life shows that the core of Christian witness consists of three constant activities:

- **Preach:** proclaim the gospel, especially its clarity about violence, oppression and injustice. Show Jesus in action in the human community, by story and example. Every Christian embodies and models Christ—and therefore "preaches."

- **Accompaniment and support:** build communities of solidarity and social engagement; encourage sharing of resources; set up a space for the families of the disappeared to share information and recover their

Gillian T.W. Ahlgren

loved ones (encourage truth-telling and commissions that lead to accountability).

- **Prophetic action:** denounce violence; strengthen and encourage goodness; be a "voice of the voiceless;" shine a light on oppression and atrocity so that it might be known, stopped, and prevented; encourage conversion.

As you consider your own life and the life of the Christian community you are a part of, how are you participating in the above activities? What more can you do? How are you making yourself replaceable in the life of the Christian community?

Metanoia Then and Now

Four lives, four very different personalities, four ways of being faithful to the gospel and collaborating with God to make the world more loving and humane: how do these faces of metanoia speak to us today? Do we find ourselves moved with admiration at their courage and tenacity, stirred to action at their example, or overwhelmed by what fidelity and integrity can sometimes cost?

It is ironic that Dorothy Day, who wrote "We are all called to be saints… and we might as well get over our bourgeois fear of the name" nonetheless cringed when she herself was called "saintly," responding "You won't make me irrelevant that easily!" Perhaps the most important lesson we can derive from the lives of these visionary leaders is that holiness, whatever else it might be, is an unfolding life-with-God that reveals itself over time, not through imitation of others, but through fidelity to what is uniquely ours to do, with God, in this world. And when a word like "holiness" seems impossible, foreign, or even downright unattractive to us, authenticity can serve as a reasonable synonym. Key for all of us (Francis, Clare, Dorothy and Oscar included) are honesty, sincerity, and time spent with God—all of which are central to our knowing and having confidence in the path that leads to a fruitful life.

The lives of our four figures demonstrate how a growing partnership with God helps us to navigate the challenges of living in a troubled world while still shedding light on what needs to change and inspiring others to collaborate in the work of making the world a home for all. Their lives also show that the trajectory of relationship with God is neither pre-ordained nor obvious—even when that relationship is strong and deep. The complexity of life and our aspirations toward goodness demand our consistent attention, attunement, and care—as well as our willingness to pivot and make changes when appropriate.

At times, we will feel so empowered by the strength of our relationship with God that we hardly notice these demands. At other times, we struggle, falter or stagnate. Consistent prayer, with dedication to listening to and integrating the counsel and wisdom of the Spirit, is critical—as is our willingness to recognize that, at times, our own perceptions and instincts are insufficient. A theme threaded through each of the lives of the visionary figures explored in this volume is how they continually chose to consult with, turn toward, and be with God, in all spaces of their lives. In prioritizing time with God, they had come to know that relationship as a wellspring of wisdom, courage, and support from which they would find what they needed to meet the challenges of daily life. Will we, too, learn to lean into our own need for God's counsel and guidance, and discover God's generous and steadfast presence?

Perhaps, as a final exercise in considering what metanoia might look like today, we could map out the moments and ways that we have known God, together with the people and places that have witnessed or facilitated those moments. Where have we sensed invitations to something beyond the surface of our lives, and how have we responded? What have we glimpsed or been prompted to notice, and is there anything that needs deeper attention? How can we choose more deeply toward our relationship with God, and free ourselves to express the love that God makes us capable of? How is your life one more example of the life-changing love that God wants to extend into the world through you?

Gillian T. W. Ahlgren

As we consider our world today—the damages that the planet and its peoples have suffered and the complex needs of the human community—it is clear enough that we have gone wrong, as a human community and as a species, in what we prioritize, how we work together (or don't), and what we are creating, for ourselves and for generations to come. The examples provided by Francis, Clare, Dorothy, and Oscar show us not only that we can change course, but also that God waits and longs for us to do so. Their models of metanoia suggest that, in engaging the depths of our relationship with God, we will be given the creativity, courage and integrity that life with God bestows on us in order to find our way.

Bibliography

Resources on Metanoia and Conversion:

Gillian T. W. Ahlgren, *The Tenderness of God: Reclaiming Our Humanity.* Fortress, 2017.

Greg Boyle, *Barking to the Choir: The Power of Radical Kinship.* Simon and Schuster, 2018.

_____, *The Whole Language: The Power of Extravagant Tenderness.* Simon and Schuster, 2021.

Pope Francis, *Gaudate et exsultate: On the Call to Holiness in Today's World.* 2017.

Bernard Lonergan, *Insight: Collected Works of Bernard Lonergan,* eds. Frederick Crowe and Robert Doran. University of Toronto Press, 1992.

Albert Nolan, *Jesus before Christianity.* Orbis Books, 1989.

Jon Sobrino, *Spiritual Writings,* ed. Robert Lassalle-Klein. Orbis Books, 2018.

Resources on Francis of Assisi:

Francis of Assisi, The Saint, The Founder, and The Prophet, collected works ed. Regis J. Armstrong. New City Press, 1999, 2000, 2001.

Michael F. Cusato, *Francis of Assisi: His Life, Vision and Companions.* Reaktion Books, 2013.

André Vauchez, *Francis of Assisi: The Life and Afterlife of a Medieval Saint*, trans. Michael F. Cusato. Yale University Press, 2013.

Resources on Clare of Assisi:

Clare of Assisi, The Lady: Early Documents, ed. Regis Armstrong. New City Press, 2006.

Ilia Delio, *Clare of Assisi: A Heart Full of Love.* Franciscan Media, 2007.

Joan Mueller, *The Privilege of Poverty: Clare of Assisi, Agnes of Prague, and the Struggle for a Franciscan Rule for Women.* Pennsylvania State University Press, 2006.

Resources on Dorothy Day:

Dorothy Day, *From Union Square to Rome.* Orig. pub. 1938. Available online at https://catholicworker.org/dorothy-day/dorothy-day-writing/

_____, *House of Hospitality*. New York: Sheed and Ward, 1939. Available online at https://catholicworker.org/dorothy-day/dorothy-day-writing/

_____, *Loaves and Fishes.* Harper and Row, 1965.

_____, *The Long Loneliness.* Orig. pub. 1952. Harper Press, 1996.

_____, *The Reckless Way of Love: Notes on Following Jesus*, ed. Carolyn Kurtz. Plough Publishing, 2017.

By Little and by Little: Selected Writings of Dorothy Day, ed. Robert Ellsberg. New York: Albert A. Knopf, 1983.

Robert Coles, *Dorothy Day: A Radical Devotion*. Grand Central Publishing, 1989.

Jim Forest, *All is Grace: A Biography of Dorothy Day*. Orbis Books, 2011.

D. L. Mayfield, *Unruly Saint: Dorothy Day's Radical Vision and Its Challenges for Our Times*. Broadleaf Books, 2022.

Terrence Wright, *Dorothy Day: An Introduction to Her Life and Thought*. Ignatius Press, 2018.

Resources on Oscar Romero:

Oscar Romero, *A Shepherd's Diary*, trans. Irene Hodgson. Franciscan Media, 1993.

_____, *The Violence of Love*, ed. James R. Brockman. Harper and Row, 1988.

_____, *Voice of the Voiceless: Four Pastoral Letters and Other Statements*, Orbis Books, 2020.

James R. Brockman, *Romero: A Life*. Orbis Books, 1989.

Michael E. Lee, *Revolutionary Saint: The Theological Legacy of Oscar Romero*. Orbis Books, 2018.

Jon Sobrino, *Archbishop Romero: Memories and Reflections*, trans. Robert R. Barr. Orbis Books, 1990.

About the Author

Gillian T. W. Ahlgren is Professor Emerita of Theology at Xavier University, where she began teaching in 1990. She received her Ph.D. from the University of Chicago in the History of Christianity with a specialization in the Christian mystical tradition. In addition to teaching graduate and undergraduate courses in theology, the history of Christianity, and Christian spirituality, she designs and facilitates retreats and immersive experiences that support personal and social transformation.

Faces of Metanoia is her ninth book. Her previous books include *Teresa of Avila and the Politics of Sanctity* (Cornell University Press, 1996), *Entering Teresa of Avila's Interior Castle: A Reader's Companion* (Paulist Press, 2005), *The Inquisition of Francisca: A Sixteenth-Century Visionary on Trial* (University of Chicago Press, 2005), *Enkindling Love: The Legacy of Teresa of Avila and John of the Cross* (Fortress Press, 2016), *The Tenderness of God: Reclaiming Our Humanity* (Fortress Press, 2017), *Spiritual Exercises for the 21st Century: A Workbook* (third edition VITALITY, 2025) and *Palace Within: Exploring Teresa of Avila's Interior Castle* (VITALITY, 2025). Dr. Ahlgren is internationally known for her work on the Christian mystical tradition and regularly gives public lectures, retreats and workshops on various figures in Christian spirituality and their wisdom for living today.

In addition to her work as a scholar and teacher, Dr. Ahlgren has been engaged in pastoral work at a variety of levels. After training in spiritual direction at the Center for Religious Development in 2005, she began to design and facilitate retreats, especially with those at the margins. In 2009 she was a founding member of the Cincinnati Women's Team of the Ignatian Spirituality Project, a national organization providing spiritual accompaniment for formerly homeless women in recovery from substance abuse. Since 2013 she has incorporated wisdom from Teresa's Interior Castle and other classic spiritual texts in her work with women who have survived domestic violence.

Dr. Ahlgren is available to facilitate workshops, training programs, immersions, and retreats. She periodically offers week-long Spiritual Immersion Experiences in the Footsteps of Francis and Clare in Assisi, in the Footsteps of Teresa in Avila, and in the Spiritual Exercises.

Please visit her website at **www.gillianahlgren.com** or contact her at **ahlgren@xavier.edu**.

Contemplative
Wisdom for
Today

About Contemplative Wisdom for Today

Contemplative Wisdom for Today is a series dedicated to making the wisdom of the Christian mystical tradition accessible as a source of practical wisdom for life today. Using the lives and teachings of visionary leaders in Christian spirituality, we support spiritual growth through reading circles, workshops, and even offer spiritual immersion experiences in Assisi, Avila, Norwich, and Santiago de Compostela. For more information, please visit **www.contemplativewisdomfortoday.org**.

Books in the Contemplative Wisdom for Today series:

Spiritual Exercises for the 21st Century: A Workbook

Palace Within: Exploring Teresa of Avila's Interior Castle

Faces of Metanoia: God's Call to Life-Changing Relationship in the Lives of Francis of Assisi, Clare of Assisi, Dorothy Day, and Oscar Romero

Transforming Habits: The Wisdom of Ignatian Spirituality for Today (forthcoming)

Three Wise Women: Clare of Assisi, Julian of Norwich, and Teresa of Avila Speak to Today (forthcoming)

VITALITY

growing love,
sharing holistic self-care,
and inspiring creative expression.

We invite you to explore with us through our
affordable, friendly drop-in classes…
in person & online

vitalitycincinnati.org

and our books

vitalitybuzz.org